PAPUA NEW GUINEA

# Social Science

## *Grade 7*

*Stephen Ranck*

Oxford University Press is a department of the University of Oxford. It furthers the University's objective of excellence in research, scholarship, and education by publishing worldwide. Oxford is a registered trademark of Oxford University Press in the UK and in certain other countries.

Published in Australia by
Oxford University Press
Level 8, 737 Bourke Street, Docklands, Victoria 3008, Australia



First published 2007
Reprinted 2008 (three times), 2009, 2010, 2012, 2014 (twice), 2015, 2017 (twice), 2019, 2021, 2023, 2025



ISBN 978 0 19 555511 0

Typeset by Palmer Higgs Pty Ltd
Illustrated by Birdwing PNG and diacriTech
Printed in Hong Kong by Sheck Wah Tong Prinitng Press Ltd.

# Contents

# Introduction

## WHAT ARE WE GOING TO DO WITH SOCIAL SCIENCE IN GRADE 7?

In this book we are going to look at the nation of Papua New Guinea and some of its neighbours for Grade 7 Social Science. You will be able to look at your own province and the entire country in this course.

You also get a chance to study Papua New Guinea and some of its neighbours. You will start to learn about some of the newest neighbours, such as Timor L'Este (East Timor), as well as about our closest neighbour, Indonesia.

We also look at some of our Pacific Island neighbours. Some of them may be familiar to you. For example, the Solomon Islands and Fiji are often in the news. Other Pacific Islands, such as Tokelau and Niue, may be new to you.

## People of our region and the environment

The studies you do in Grade 7 will build on the work you did in Grade 6. We will look at the physical and human environments in the regions around us. This includes people living in some of the smallest and most isolated nations on Earth in the Pacific Ocean. It also includes Australia, our neighbour to the south.

We will see that our different neighbours have very different environments and resources. You will need to find information about these many places. You may compare sustainable practices in Papua New Guinea and among our neighbours.

You will have the chance to work with maps and to make your own maps to study the province and the nation.

## Governments and economic development

People have many ways of organising. One type of organisation is government. Some people have colonial governments. Other people have independent governments. We will look at different types of governments. We will also look at the history of governments in Papua New Guinea and the Pacific islands.

## What is happening to culture in our region?

Some parts of cultures are changing quickly, while others are changing less quickly. And in other places, change is very slow in some things. But everywhere there are changes.

You will get to study culture and changes in the region. You will be the investigator. You will have to search for more information using the radio, newspapers, magazines, books, people and other sources you can find.

## Project work

At the end of the course, you will get to do your own social science study. Do you remember the process?

- You will start with looking at something that interests you about people in your province or in Papua New Guinea or in the region.
- This leads you to an idea or a question that you can study and test.
- You will gather information about your idea.
- You will question what is true and what is false from the information you gather.
- You will remember about bias and prejudice and try to avoid it by studying all sides of the question.
- You will write up a report.
- You will make a conclusion about what is true and what was not true in your study.
- The conclusion should help you to know what will happen in the future.

At the end of the Grade 7 Social Science course, you should know much more about the region and about the roles of Papua New Guinea and your province. Enjoy the studies ahead. There is much to learn. And something of interest is there for everyone.

Throughout this book you will see key words in **bold** type. You can find these words and their definitions in the Glossary at the back of this book.

# Environment and Resources

## Chapter summary

In this chapter you will have the opportunity to:

✓ investigate the physical and human environments of your province, the nation and region

✓ investigate how the physical environment influences human settlements in your province, the nation and region

✓ investigate the impact of resource use in provincial, national and neighbouring regions of the human environment

✓ describe national and regional sustainable practices

✓ investigate hazardous natural events in Papua New Guinea and neighbouring regions.

## Syllabus references

**Syllabus strand:** Environment and Resources

**Syllabus sub-strand:** People and environment: Papua New Guinea and the region

Outcomes

**7.1.1** Students are able to identify and describe human and physical environments of the province, nation and region, and describe the factors and processes that have formed them

**7.1.2** Students are able to describe how national physical environments influence human settlement patterns in the nation and neighbouring regions

**7.1.3** Students are able to describe the impact of resource use on physical environments and human settlement patterns in provincial, national and neighbouring regions

**7.1.4** Students are able to describe national and regional sustainable practices related to the natural environment, and propose possible solutions to problems

**7.1.5** Students are able identify and describe the causes and effects of hazardous natural events in Papua New Guinea and neighbouring regions, and how people respond to them

# Papua New Guinea and neighbours: The physical environment

In the chapter, we will first look at Papua New Guinea and the **region**. You will discover what the main physical features are. We will use maps to help us. You can review map reading skills. Then we will look at the history of the main physical features. You will learn how **islands** and mountains are made.

We will then move from the physical environment to the human environment. We will look at the main parts of the human environment.

## THE ISLAND OF NEW GUINEA

**New Guinea** is the second largest island in the world. The island of New Guinea covers more than 791 000 square kilometres of land. Greenland is the largest island in the world. Australia is an island continent. That is even larger.

Papua New Guinea is made up of islands and **ocean**. The two biggest parts of the physical environment are land and sea. It is important to take care of both of them. The mainland of Papua New Guinea is half of the island of New Guinea. The whole island has some shared physical features.

Look at the map of New Guinea on the inside back cover. A series of mountains runs east to west across New Guinea. Sometimes people call this a spine or backbone of mountains running across the island. In the central part of New Guinea there are wide valleys. The valleys are narrower at the eastern and western ends of the island. The eastern and western ends of the island mountain chain have narrow, steep valleys. You will find a very big swamp in the southwest of the island.

## For you to try

- Look at the map of New Guinea on the inside back cover. Discuss the physical features you see. Why do you think people refer to the mountains as a spine or backbone? Are there any other parts of New Guinea that can be described as part of a body?
- What other physical features do you see? What are the island's main physical features?

## Location: Where are we?

First, let us review some basic information about maps. We use four basic directions to locate places. These are called the four **cardinal points** of the compass: north, south, east and west.

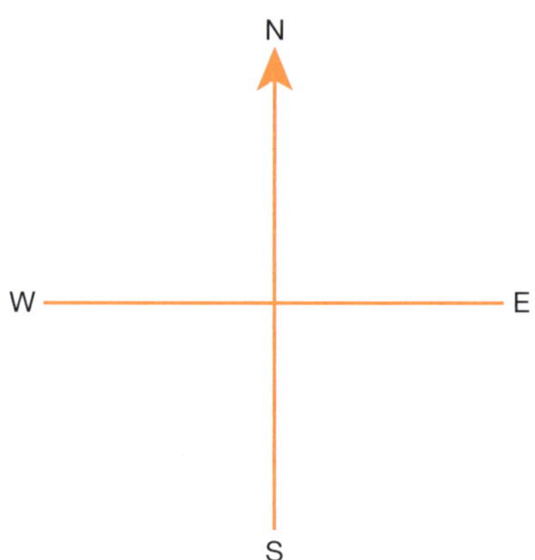


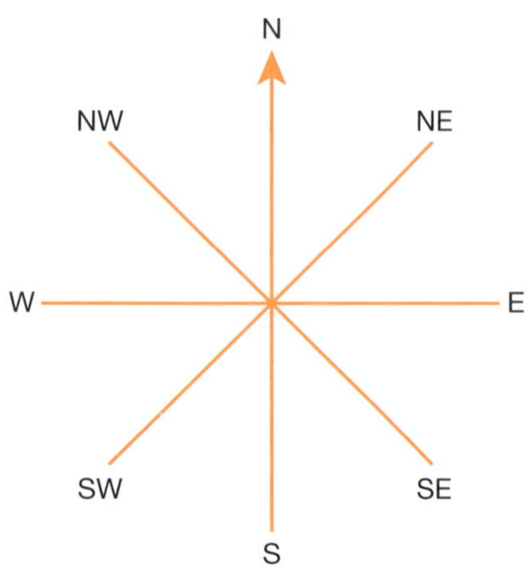


From these four points we can make a compass rose (like a flower). We have now added northeast, northwest, southeast and southwest to the original four compass points.

Maps help us with locations. The map of the island of New Guinea tells us about the location of physical features on the island. Different maps can give different types of information. We need a regional map to tell us where Papua New Guinea is compared to other countries in our region. Look at the regional map on the inside front cover of this book. You will see that Papua New Guinea is surrounded by neighbours and water, and that it is in the South Pacific Ocean.

## For you to try

- Look at the regional map on the inside front cover. What is north of Papua New Guinea? What is to the east? The south? And finally, what is to the west?
- Can you locate Port Moresby? It is not shown on the map because the **scale** is too small. You should know approximately where it is. Can you estimate how far it is from Port Moresby to Sydney, Australia? How far from Port Moresby to Fiji? And how far from Port Moresby to the Hawaiian Islands?

The eastern half of New Guinea is the independent nation of Papua New Guinea. It includes the mainland and three large outlying islands. These islands are New Britain, New Ireland and Bougainville (or North Solomons). As well, there are many smaller islands. Papua New Guinea's total land area is about 463 000 square kilometres. The total territory including the sea is over two million square kilometres.

Our land provides food, our homes and our clothes. Our sea provides food, transportation and cooling water. Which do you think is more important?

## For you to try

- List as many of Papua New Guinea's islands as you can name.
- After you have made your list, divide into two teams and debate the following: "The most important part of an island is the water that surrounds it" *versus* "The most important part of an island is the land that makes the island."

## Physical features of Papua New Guinea

The land of Papua New Guinea changes from place to place, but generally it is very rugged and mountainous. The mountains are steep and many rivers pour down from them. Look at the map of New Guinea on the inside back cover. You will see that mountains run from one end of Papua New Guinea to the other. Other landforms include raised coral reefs, alluvial plains, swamps, coastal plains, glacial landscapes and volcanic landforms.

Papua New Guinea shares a long land and sea **border** with **Indonesia.** The other half of the island of New Guinea contains several Indonesian **provinces.**

## For you to try

- There are many political differences between Papua New Guinea and **West Papua**, Indonesia. Are there many differences in the physical geography? How are they similar? Would you expect them to have the same type of physical **resources**?
- Now go back to the regional map on the inside front cover. What about the other Pacific islands? Looking at them, what sort of physical geographies do you think we shall find?

## Climate

Climate is the term we use when we talk about the weather in a certain place over a long period of time. Papua New Guinea is located within the humid tropics. That means that the climate is generally warm and wet. But in the highest mountains of the Indonesian part of New Guinea, it can be very cold, with snow and ice.

## For you to try

- Look at the climate map of Papua New Guinea below. What are the five main types of climate? Discuss the types of climates in your province.
- Compare the climate map with the physical map of New Guinea. You will only be able to compare the parts that cover Papua New Guinea. Discuss the physical features that are related to climate. What do you think the two most important physical features are for climates?

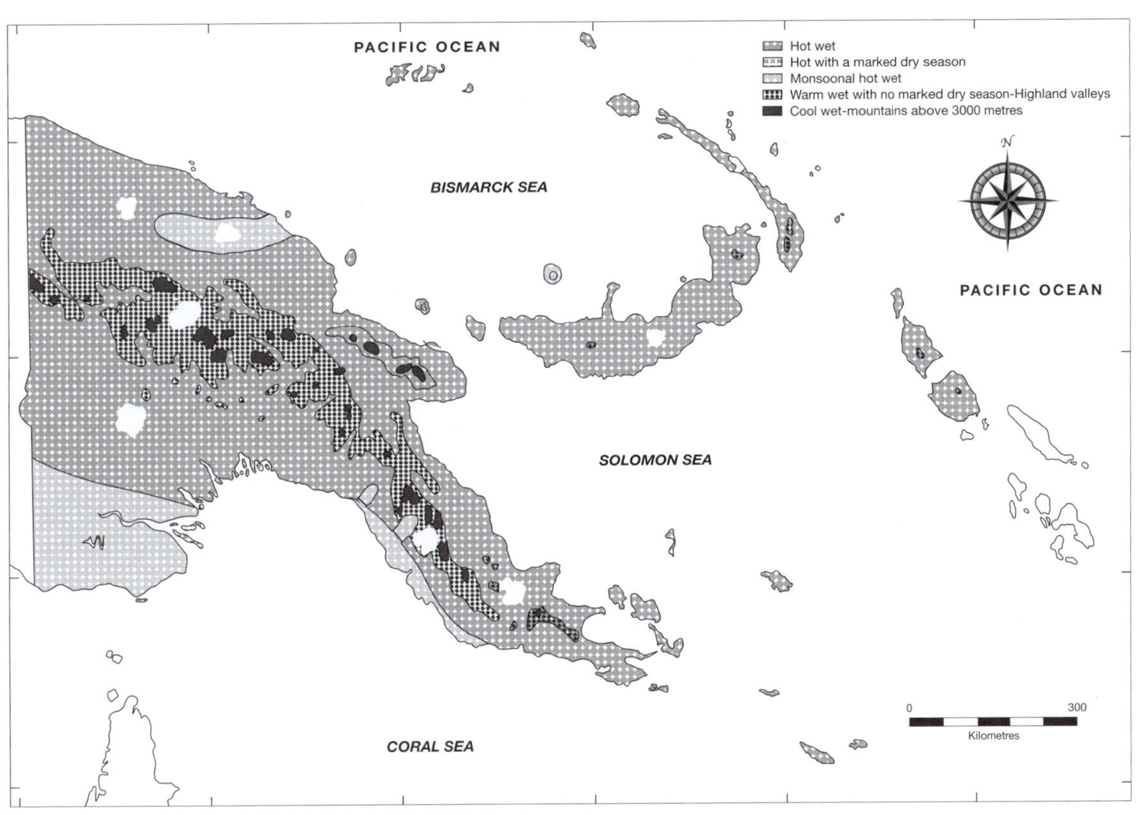

## Vegetation

Much of Papua New Guinea is still covered by forest. Forest vegetation changes with elevation. Lowland forest is found along the coast and other low-lying areas. Much of this has been cut by loggers. Lowland forest trees reach up to 40 metres high in a mature forest.

At about 1000 metres of elevation, lowland forest starts to become lower mountain forest with shorter trees than found in the lowland forest. In valleys of the Highlands, much of this forest has been cut down for gardens.

The upper mountain forest has even smaller trees. It starts at around 3000 metres and finishes around 3900 metres. Trees may only be two to five metres tall.

On some of the dryer coastal parts of Papua New Guinea, the natural vegetation is savannah. This is grassland mixed with trees. Some of these savannah trees are eucalyptus. All of them are also found in Australia.

Grasslands are a major feature of much of the Highlands. These are caused mainly by human changes to the original vegetation. Another human vegetation feature is garden and other agricultural vegetation. This can be found from sea level to about 2700 metres.

Freshwater and saltwater swamps are another major type of vegetation in parts of Papua New Guinea. Many of the coastal provinces have some major swampland. Saltwater swamps are often mangrove swamps. The mangrove trees provide a good environment for fish to breed.

## For you to try

- Determine what the major vegetation types are in your province. Compare your province's vegetation with the vegetation of another province.
- What is the vegetation in your province good for? Can it be used as a resource to sell to other provinces or other countries?

## Other Pacific islands and close neighbours

There are many other Pacific island countries. The regional map on the inside front cover of this book shows many of them. You can see that Papua New Guinea is large compared to many of them.

The north sea border of Papua New Guinea reaches the equator. The south border reaches 12 degrees south on the map. Australia is south of Papua New Guinea. The Indonesian archipelago is west of Papua New Guinea. **Archipelago** means a group of many islands. The nation of Indonesia has 13 000 islands.

The Pacific Ocean surrounds Papua New Guinea. It is a very large body of water and is the largest ocean in the world. Many small island countries are in the Pacific.

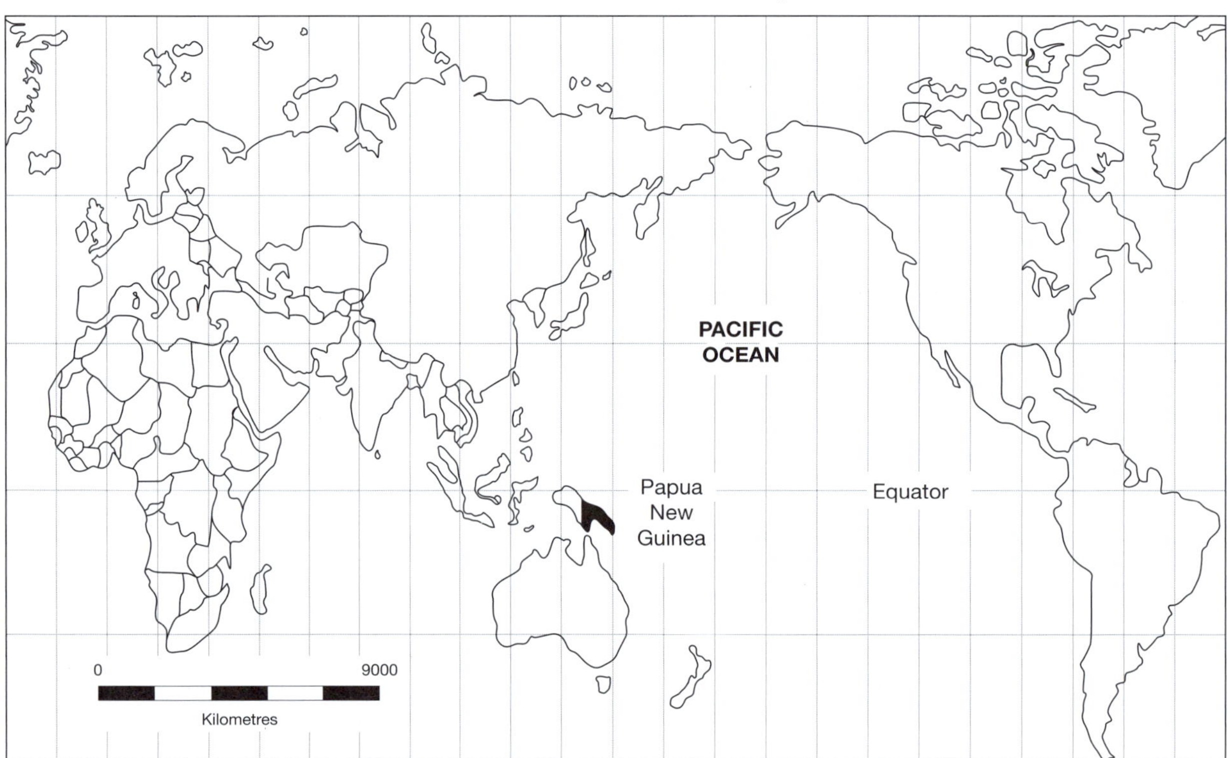

The Pacific Ocean covers one-third of the world's surface. It covers nearly 153 million square kilometres. This is a big space. Some scientists used to think the moon was torn out from the Earth and that left the space for the Pacific Ocean. Now scientists have a better explanation for the Pacific Ocean. We shall discuss that in another section later on.

The Pacific Ocean has the deepest parts of all oceans. Some places are nearly 11 000 metres deep. Islands in the Pacific Ocean are often the tops of mountains. These would be the tallest mountains in the world if the water were taken away.

The Pacific Ocean contains about 645 million cubic kilometres of water. This is nearly as much as all the other oceans in the world combined. The average depth of the Pacific Ocean is about 4300 metres.

The closer a place is to the equator, the warmer the climate will be. Another factor is elevation or altitude. The higher the altitude the cooler the climate becomes. The ocean acts to moderate temperatures. This means that the water changes temperature slowly. Places on the coast or smaller islands are influenced by the sea temperatures. Inland on large islands, temperatures can change more quickly.

## For you to try

- Look at the regional map on the inside front cover. How many Pacific island countries can you locate? Are there other ones you know of that are missing from the regional map?
- What do you think the climate would be like on some of the smaller islands you can see on the regional map?

# How was the island of New Guinea formed?

The history of New Guinea covers millions of years. In fact, the land you are now on travelled for millions of years before people moved to New Guinea. Scientists think that hundreds of millions of years ago, all the land in the world was together. This was one gigantic landmass or *plate*, a part of the Earth's rigid crust. The rest of the world was covered by sea. This single landmass was surrounded by that sea.

About 200 million years ago, that single landmass began to break apart, first into two plates, then into more parts. These plates travelled. New Guinea and Australia slowly travelled together for millions of years. They travelled very slowly at two to five centimetres a year.

## The movement of land

For many years, scientists could not understand how the very large land masses could move across the Earth. The best explanation now is that the thin crust of the Earth is floating on molten material that behaves like a liquid. Sometimes this liquid escapes to the surface of the Earth. This is when lava, molten rock, comes out. It then hardens like the rest of the surface.

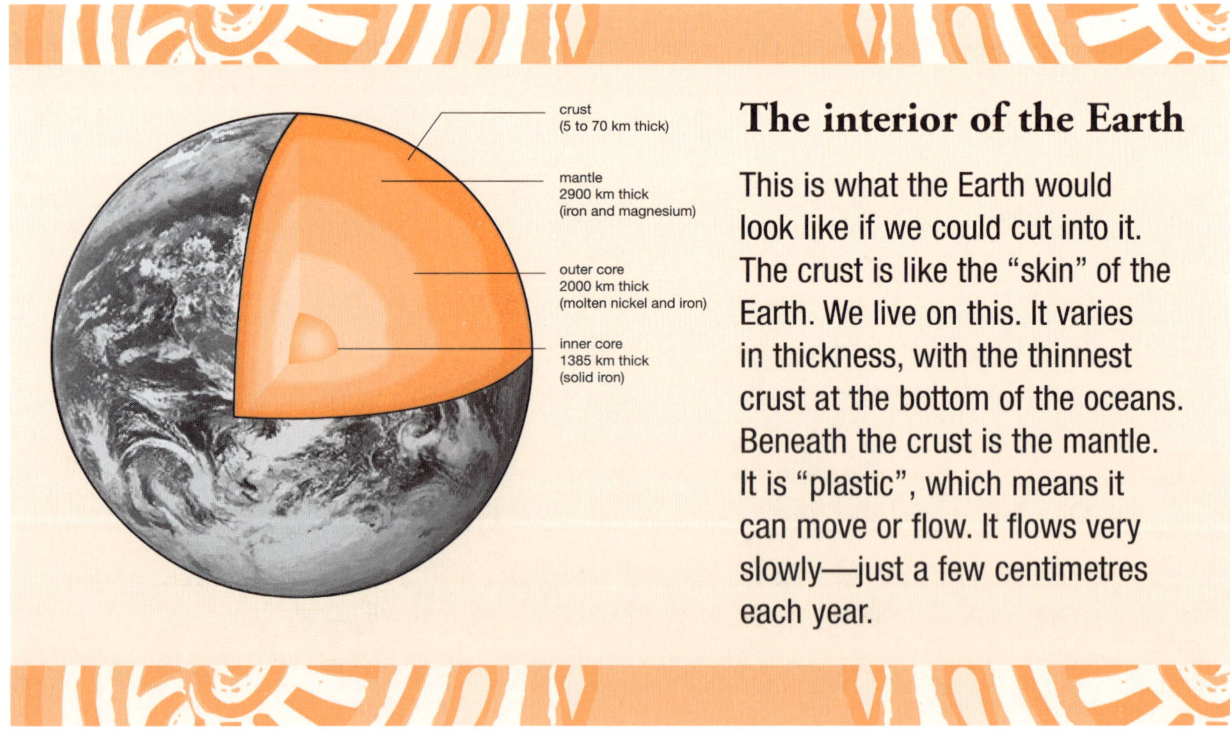


### The interior of the Earth

This is what the Earth would look like if we could cut into it. The crust is like the "skin" of the Earth. We live on this. It varies in thickness, with the thinnest crust at the bottom of the oceans. Beneath the crust is the mantle. It is "plastic", which means it can move or flow. It flows very slowly—just a few centimetres each year.

Different parts of the Earth's crust have broken into plates. These are called *tectonic plates*. New Guinea and Australia are on the same plate. New Caledonia, New Zealand and Fiji are on this plate too. For 200 million years they have been travelling around two to five centimetres a year.

You can see where they now are on the regional map. Look at them and imagine that they were once all together. They were one part of a single large landmass. We call that super continent Pangaea. Pangaea started to separate into two landmasses, called Laurasia and Gondwanaland, about 200 million years ago. These separated again into more tectonic plates. Many scientists think that tectonic plates have all come together and broken apart before Pangaea started to break up 200 million years ago. This took hundreds of millions of years each time.

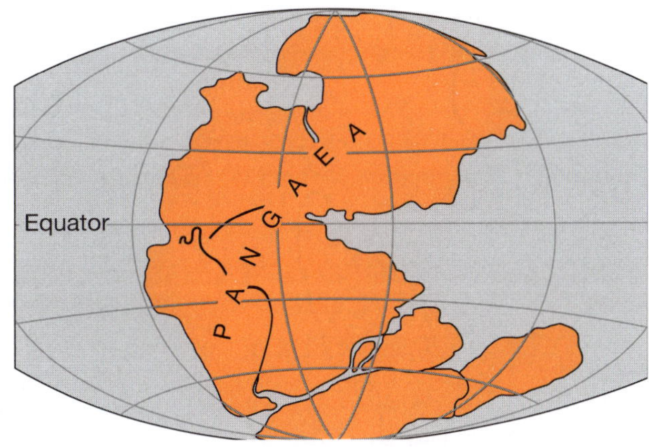


Pangaea (225 million years ago)

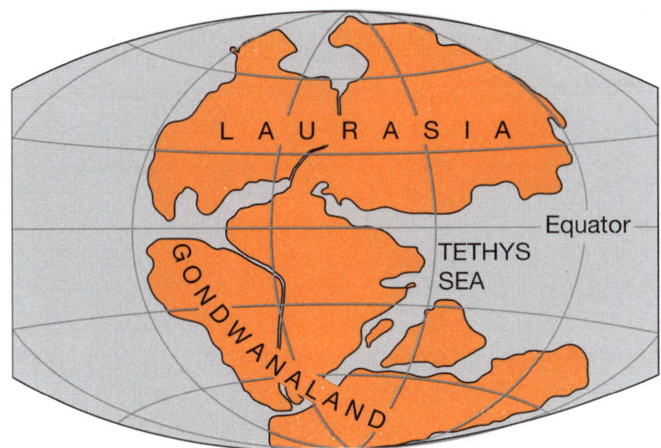


Lauasia and Gondwanaland (200 million years ago)

Tectonic plates push against each other. The edge of one plate goes up and the other plate slowly slides underneath. This is one way mountains are made. Sometimes this is a slow process, but sometimes it is very fast and violent. This can cause earthquakes, volcanoes and other physical activities. New Guinea and parts of Indonesia are on the edge of plates. This is why they have mountains, earthquakes and volcanoes.

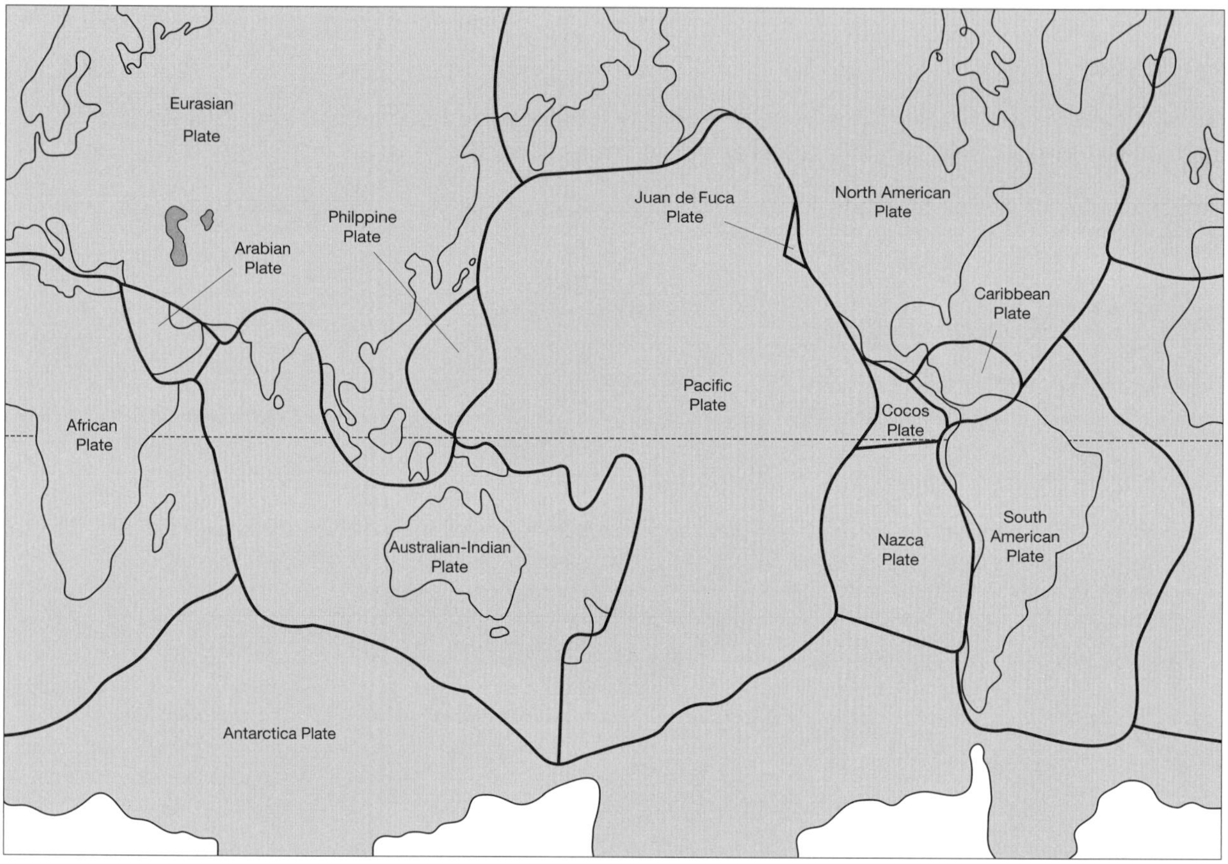

Tectonic plates

## For you to try

- Discuss tectonic plates with the class. Consider that right now Australia and Papua New Guinea are moving between two and five centimetres each year. Will all the continents come together again? Did the plates move before 200 million years ago?
- What do you think New Guinea will be like if the plates all come together again in another 100 million years?

## What is an island?

An island is land that is entirely surrounded by water but is smaller than a continent. Some islands are very big.

| The four largest islands in the world | |
|---|---|
| **Island** | **Area in square kilometres** |
| Greenland | 2 170 000 |
| New Guinea | 792 500 |
| Borneo | 725 500 |
| Madagascar | 587 000 |

There are four large sets of Pacific Ocean islands: Papua New Guinea, New Zealand, Fiji and New Caledonia. These are called *continental islands*. They were once part of the early southern continent of Gondwana. They are fragments that are now surrounded by ocean. All of them have volcanic activity. They are all near the boundaries of the Australian and Pacific tectonic plates.

Many other Pacific islands are small or very small. We can group islands in many ways. Most of the smaller Pacific islands are called *oceanic islands*. They are hundreds of kilometres away from continents. Most have been created by volcanic activity. The size means that the physical geography will be limited. We can look at a selection of them.

**Niue**: The land area of Niue is only 261 square kilometres. The nation of Niue is one of the world's largest coral islands. There are steep limestone cliffs all along the coast, and a coral reef surrounds the island.

**Fiji**: The nation of Fiji is made up of 332 islands. The total land area is 18 333 square kilometres. There are many coral islands and other islands. The two largest islands are Viti Levu and Vanua Levu. Both are mountainous and have areas of good soil. Coral islands do not have good soil.

**Kiribati**: Kiribati (pronounced *Kiribas*) is an island nation. Kiribati consists of 33 islands. The nation stretches several thousand kilometres across the Pacific. Most of its islands are coral islands. The Tarawa Atoll is where most I Kiribati people live. The nation of Kiribati also has the biggest coral atoll in the world. It is part of the Line Islands and named Kritimati Island. Kritimati Island is also known as Christmas Island, Kiribati. Sometimes this is confused with Christmas Island in the Indian Ocean. That is a different island. But both of them are coral islands and both have many land crabs.

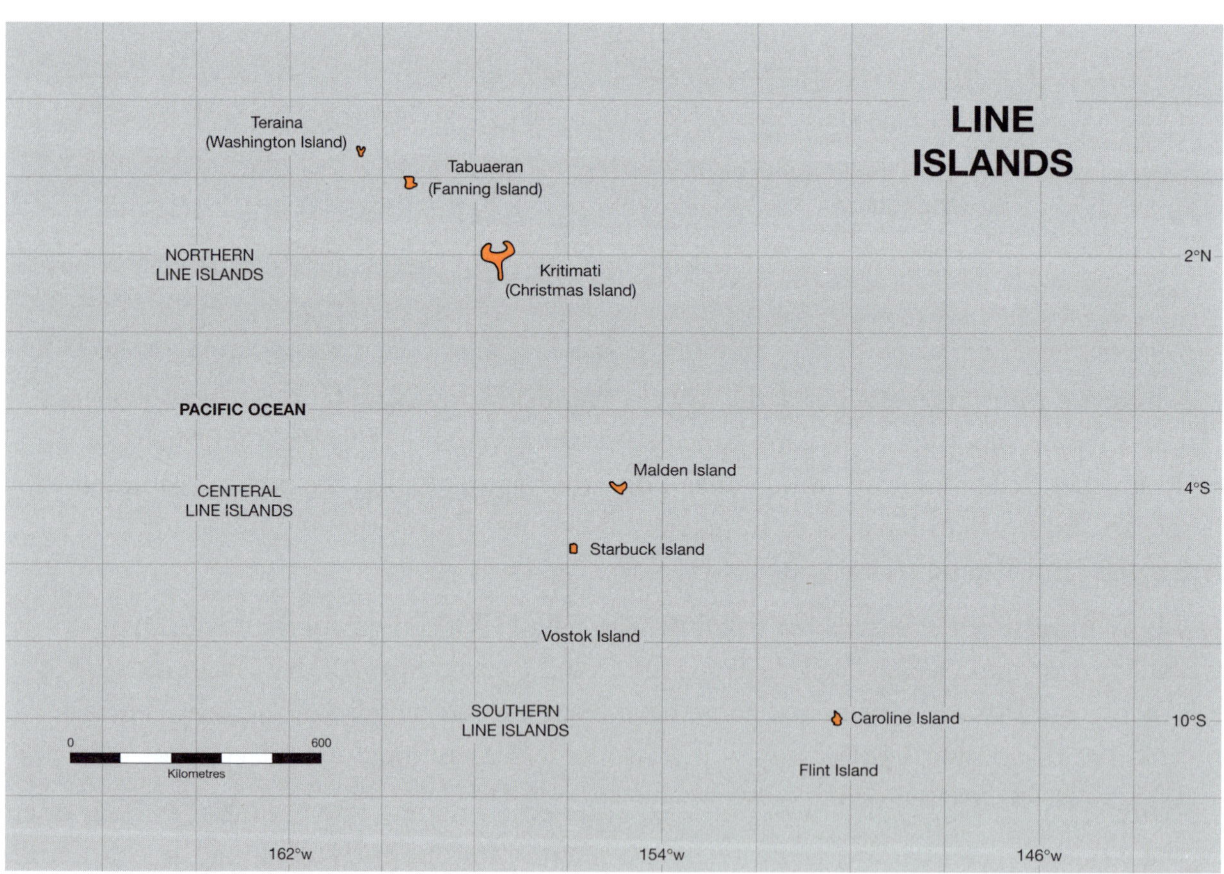

### For you to try

- Look at the regional map on the inside front cover. Can you find the Line Islands on the regional map?
- Now study the map of Kritimati Island (Christmas Island) Kiribati on page 16. What is the scale? Compare this scale to the regional map. Discuss how the differences in scale give the maps different uses. Divide into groups and see how many map uses you can think of for the two different scales.

## PAPUA NEW GUINEA AND THE PACIFIC ISLANDS: THE HUMAN ENVIRONMENT

The Pacific islands have nearly all filled with people. People create a human environment wherever they settle. Humans make up boundaries. We have looked at some of these as part of the maps of the physical environment.

Boundaries and other features define different parts of the human environment. We can map towns, cities, roads and cash crops to show parts of the human environment. There are many other examples.

Papua New Guinea is divided into provinces. The provincial map of Papua New Guinea below shows provincial boundaries and the capital of each province.

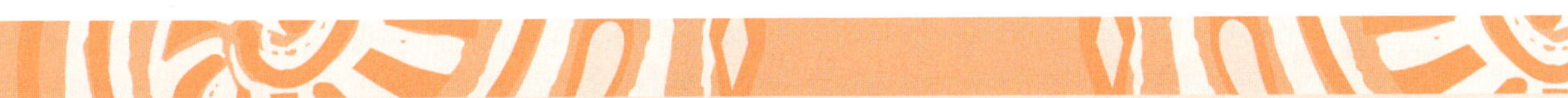

Make a large copy of the provincial map of Papua New Guinea on the next page. (Do not write on the map in this textbook. You will need this map many times for different work.) You may want to draw it with a strong outline. You will start to put new information on it. You will draw lightly to be able to correct mistakes. Use different symbols, colours or lines for different items. If there is no paper to make a copy on, you can use the blackboard and work as a group.

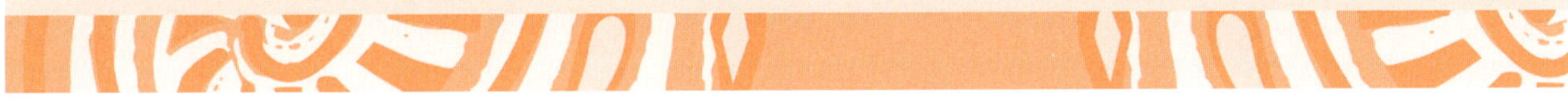

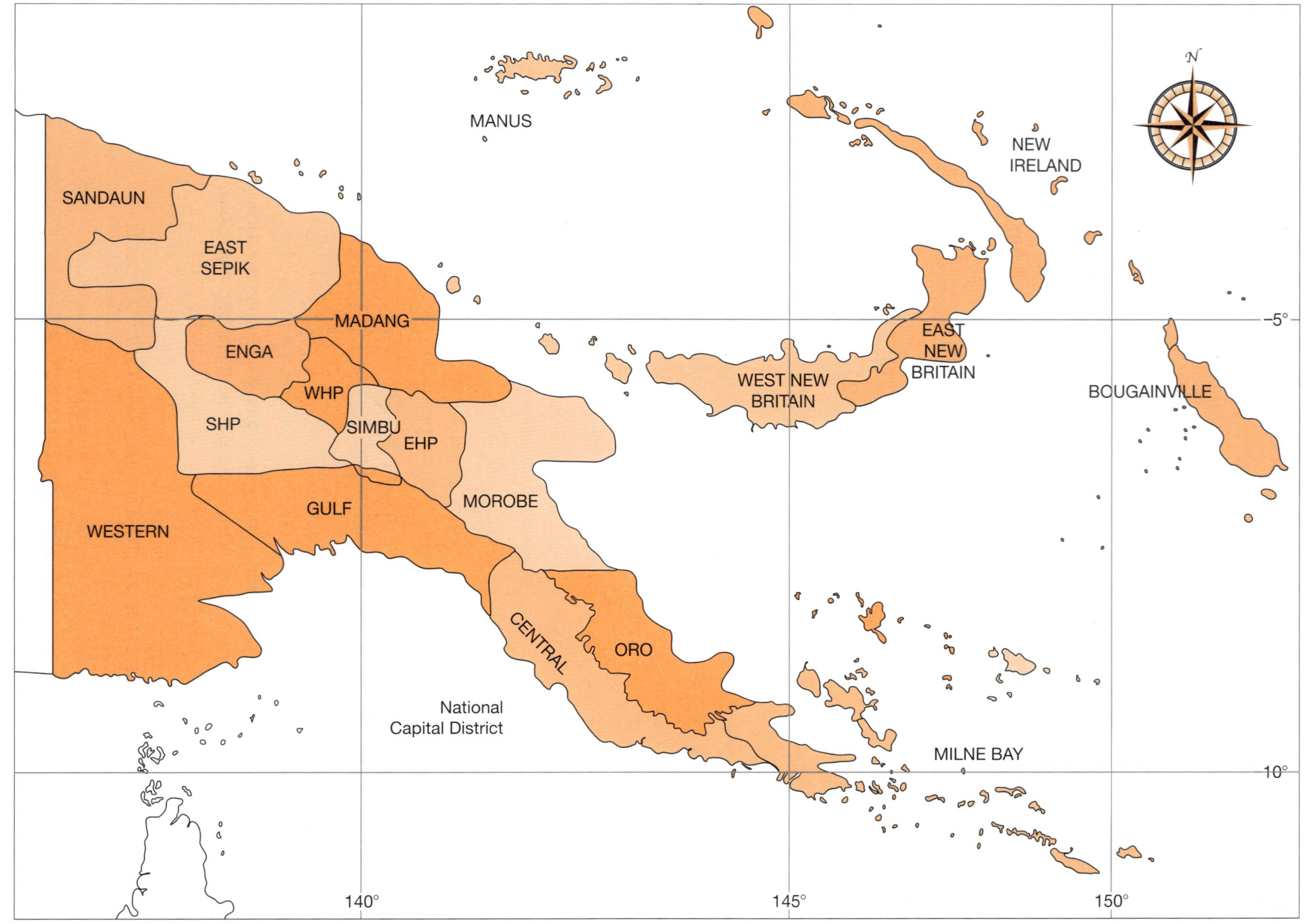
MANUS
NEW IRELAND
N
SANDAUN
EAST SEPIK
MADANG
ENGA
WHP
SHP
SIMBU
EHP
MOROBE
WESTERN
GULF
EAST NEW BRITAIN
WEST NEW BRITAIN
BOUGAINVILLE
CENTRAL
ORO
National Capital District
MILNE BAY
-5°
10°
140°
145°
150°

## For you to try

- On your copied map, draw the major roads in Papua New Guinea and your province, major air routes, major agricultural and cash crop areas, cities and other large concentrations of people, and other parts of the human environment that you think are important.
- Make a map of your province. Use a larger scale than for the provincial map of Papua New Guinea. How many more human features can you show on this map? Discuss the major human features in your province. What kind of human environment does your province have compared to other provinces?
- Divide the class into groups. Have each group select one type of important human feature. Hold debates on which feature is most important.

# Early human settlement in our region

People have taken thousands of years to settle the Pacific islands. Where did all these people come from? No one knows the whole story. Some may have come by boat, and others may have used rafts to float between islands that were closer when the level of the sea was low.

The first settlers left no written records, but some of them did leave clues. We can see evidence of the past by looking at the language they brought, the pottery they used and their farming and fishing techniques that they shared with each other. We can also look at the **genetic** evidence that shows us the close relationships between people all over the world.

No one is sure when or how people first came to New Guinea, and there are many debates about this. Because it was a long time ago, we can never be sure. But we can make guesses based on the evidence, or clues, we have found.

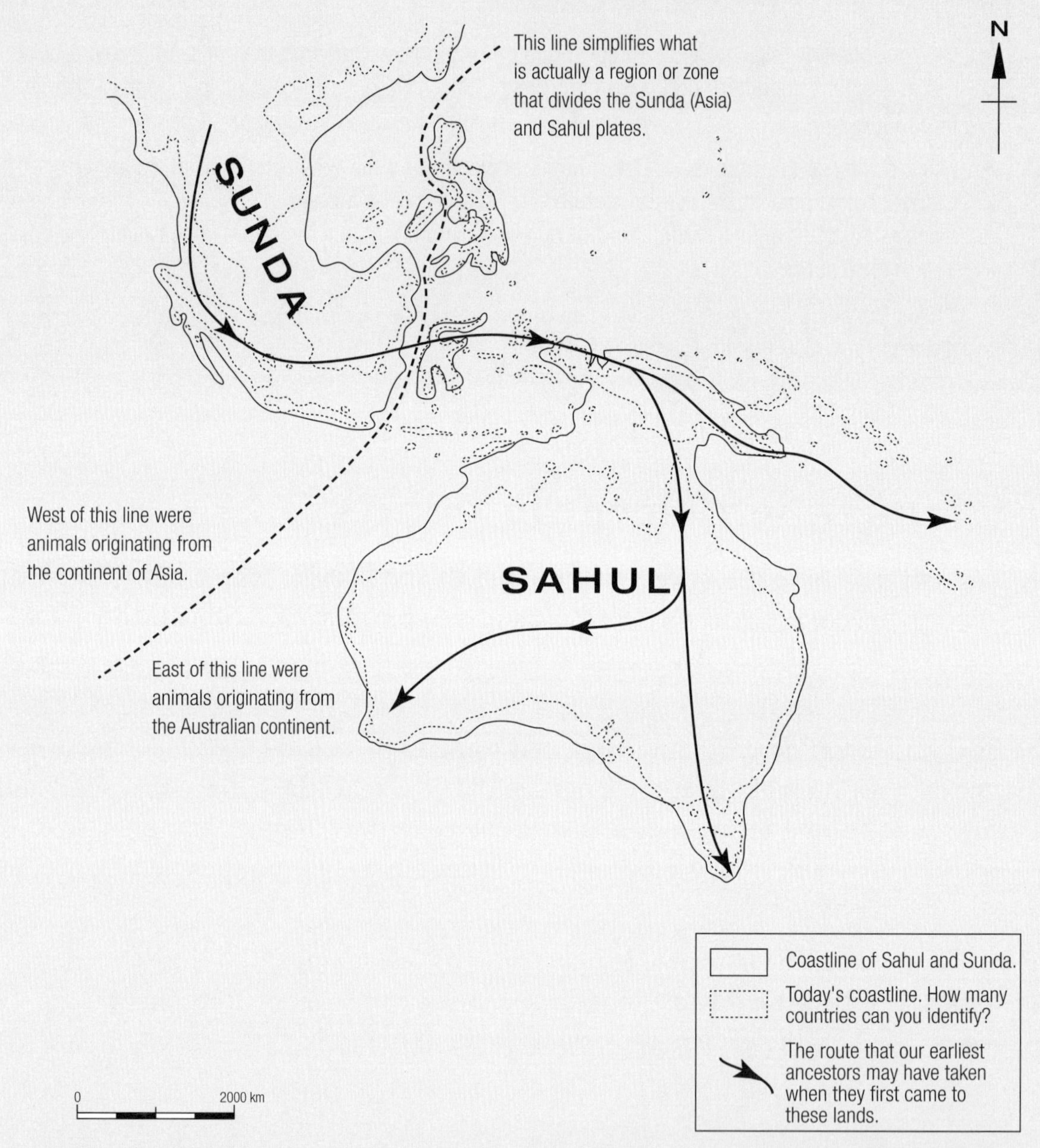


It is believed that the level of the sea was much lower many thousands of years ago, which meant that there was more land to be seen. Two larger land masses—Sunda and Sahul—might have made the migration of people and animals much easier.

Sea level rose and fell during this time. Many clues to early settlements on the coast may now be under water. People travelled around the Bismarck Archipelago and mainland Papua New Guinea for at least 35 000 years or more. Trade items like obsidian tell us this. (Obsidian is a volcanic rock, a natural glass that people used to make very sharp blades and other items.)

## Genetic evidence

Genetic evidence indicates that all present people originally came from Africa about 200 000 years ago. Modern humans now cover the whole world.

According to the genetic evidence, a group left Africa between 70 000 and 50 000 years ago. The genetic ancestors of one group are found in nearly all Australian aboriginal people. The same traces are found in Andaman Island and some Malaysian aboriginal people, and in some Papua New Guinea people. (*Aboriginal* means "from the beginning", and refers to people who were in a place many thousands of years ago. Another term for these people is *indigenous*.) The present genetic evidence indicates that people arrived in Papua New Guinea and Australia before people settled in Europe.

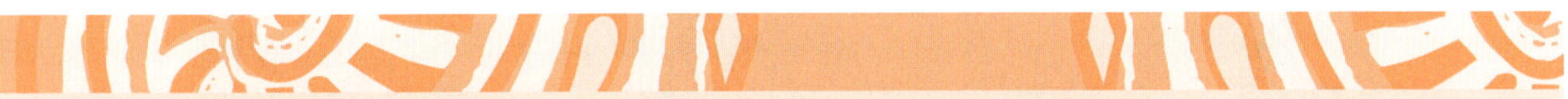

All present human beings are very closely related. The genetic make-up of all people is the same 999 times out of 1000. That means that we are all 99.9% the same. But the little differences of one in a thousand can help tell about our past.

### For you to try

- Imagine you were the first person to reach the island of New Guinea. What do you think it would have been like? What do you think your biggest problems would be?
- If you were with the very first people to come to New Guinea, what clues do you think you might have left behind to show that you settled here? How long would the clues last? How hard would the evidence be to find?
- Look at your present human settlement. Can you see any clues of older human settlements? See what information you can find in groups or individually about past settlements in your province. Ask older relatives and friends about what they know.

## Physical evidence

Physical remains of humans and animals can tell us a lot about where people lived and where they came from. Bones and fossils that are similar in far away places may give us a clue about the origins of the people or animals from which they came.

Artefacts are objects made by humans, such as tools, pottery, jewellery and weapons. They tell us a lot about how and where people lived. They can also tell us where people moved and what other groups they interacted and traded with. For example, if we find similar patterns in pottery, jewellery or fabric used by very different groups of people, we can assume that they might have had some contact in the far past and shared their technology or their ideas.

Lapita pottery gives us clues about early settlement in New Guinea.

About 4000 years ago people in the Bismarck Archipelago started making a new type of pottery called Lapita pottery. Within 200 years, this same type of pottery was found as far away as Samoa. The first known settlements in Vanuatu and New Caledonia also contain Lapita pottery.

Prehistorians discovered stone axes or blades in Sialum, on the Huon Peninsula, Morobe Province in the 1980s. They used a special process to date these tools to about 40 000 years old. They can tell the age by the way the surface has changed.

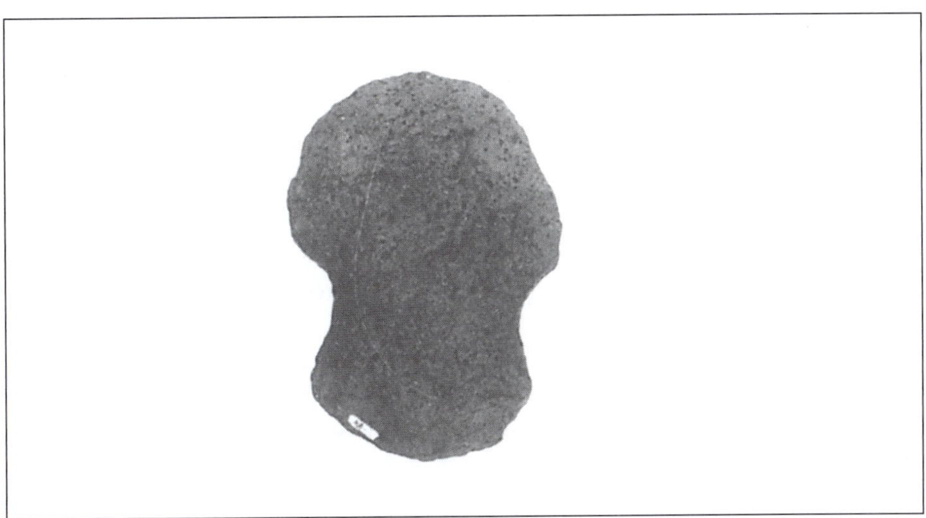

A "waisted" stone axe blade from Robogara, Sialum area, Morobe Province.

The stone is soft and the blades are large. They would be very weak axes. Maybe they were hoes. They are called waisted blades. This is because they have a scooped out "waist" (like a person). These were probably used so that a stick could be tied to the blade.

Finally, these blades were washed down to the coastal location. Maybe they have travelled a kilometre, maybe much further. Again no one is sure where they actually come from.

Obsidian stone tool, Lou Island, Manus Province.

## For you to try

- Look at the pictures of the stone tools on page 23. What do you think they were used for?
- Try making one of the tools and try to use it.

## Language evidence

Another set of clues about early settlement in the Pacific is language. In Papua New Guinea there are two major language groups. One is called Austronesian. The other major language group in Papua New Guinea is called non-Austronesian.

The Austronesian-speaking people probably came from Asia. There was an Austronesian language spoken in South East Asia around 6000 years ago. Some of these people probably came to Papua New Guinea. They needed good boat skills to get here and to continue further into the Pacific.

Austronesian is found in some coastal and some island parts of Papua New Guinea. It is also found across many other Pacific Islands. Polynesian, Hawaiian and Maori are Austronesian languages. About 15 per cent of Papua New Guinea's original languages are Austronesian. These are fairly easy languages to learn.

Some of the words around the Pacific are similar. For example, *mumu* and *umu* both mean *ground oven*, and *hahini* and *wahini* both mean *woman*. Motu is an example of an Austronesian language in Papua New Guinea. Many people have heard Motu because it was used as one of the common languages in **colonial** times.

**Comparison of some Austronesian words**

| English | Rapanui | Hawaiian | Maori |
|---|---|---|---|
| island | motu | moku | motu |
| water | rano | wai | wai |
| fish | ika | i'a | ika |
| bird | manu | manu | manu |
| banana | maika | mai'a | maiku |

The non-Austronesian languages are much more complex and difficult to learn. They make up about 85 per cent of the original languages here. They come from people who came to Papua New Guinea much earlier, but no one is sure when they arrived. They may have come to New Guinea first and then to Australia, or gone to Australia first and then to New Guinea.

No one knows where non-Austronesian languages come from. Many of them do not appear to be related to each other. All the Austronesian languages are related like a big family, but non-Austronesian languages may represent very different groups.

## For you to try

Look at the regional and Papua New Guinea maps in this book. Find the following places where Austronesian languages are spoken: Hawaii, New Zealand, Samoa, Tokelau, Wallis and Futuna, Lou Island (Papua New Guinea), Misima Island (Papua New Guinea).

- From the examples, what sort of an area does the Austronesian language cover in the Pacific?
- How far did people have to travel to spread these languages? What would they need to travel so far?
- How would they survive when they got to an island? What must they have brought with them?

## How did people get to Remote Oceania?

People have been around New Guinea and the Bismarck Archipelago for tens of thousands of years. Beyond this to the east are the large areas of Pacific Ocean. There is no evidence that people started to settle the smaller islands of the Central Pacific until about 3800 years ago. So who were the first people there? Scientists have a few ideas. Look at three of them and then discuss what you think happened.

1. Many scientists think that the people who knew how to make Lapita pottery were the first explorers of Remote Oceania, the name we have given to the distant islands of the Pacific. The most remote islands from Papua New Guinea and the Solomon Islands are Hawaii to the north, New Zealand to the south and Easter Island, which is far to the southeast from us. Some scientists have thought that the Lapita pottery people came to New Guinea four or five thousand years ago. They had better boats and gardening skills. They settled on the Aru Islands and other parts of the Bismarck Archipelago. Then some of them went to Remote Oceania, which is towards the centre of the Pacific.

2. Other scientists have thought that the Lapita people knew how to garden. The people before them would have had good boats. Maybe some explored parts of the Pacific but they did not have the garden resources to stay in Remote Oceania. The Lapita people had gardening skills and brought plants with them to islands that had very few garden foods. They knew that islands existed far away and planned missions to settle them.

3. Another set of scientists have thought that the people who made Lapita pottery were part of the people in New Guinea for a long time. Some of them took the gardening and boat skills to explore the Pacific.

No one knows what the right answer is. All we can do is to look at the clues and the evidence.

## The evidence

- There is physical evidence of human settlement on the far north coast of Australia from about 50 000 years ago.
- There is also evidence of people buried at Lake Mungo in the south east of Australia 45 000 years ago. And there are artefacts in soil that is 50 000 years old at Lake Mungo. Maybe people were there 50 000 years ago.
- There are many places with evidence of people being in Australia 30 000 to 20 000 years ago.
- Stone tools have been found at Sialum on the Huon Peninsula in Papua New Guinea that are 40 000 years old. They provide evidence of people but no one is sure where the settlement actually was or what the tools were used for.
- There is evidence of people on the Bismarck Archipelago, which includes New Britain, New Ireland, Manus and Buka, from 35 000 to 20 000 years ago.
- Evidence of humans using fire as a tool in the Highlands 32 000 years ago.
- The earliest people reached as far as parts of the Solomon Islands 35 000 years ago. There is no physical evidence for these people reaching the more distant islands of the Pacific that long ago.
- There is evidence of people 25 000 years ago at Kosipe and Nombe in Central Province. Scientists have found stone tools at these locations.
- There is evidence of people with an extensive agricultural system at Kuk in the Western Highlands Province possibly as early as 9000 years ago.

## For you to try

- Measure the distances on the regional map between the different islands of the Bismarck Archipelago (including New Britain, New Ireland, Manus and Buka) and New Guinea. Estimate how far people travelled.
- Next, measure the distances between the Solomon Islands, New Caledonia and Vanuatu. How much farther did people have to go?

## New and changing clues

Evidence and clues about early human settlement change. New research will give more clues to the early settlement of the Pacific and Papua New Guinea. A new science now used is genetics. The study of genetics may give many more clues about early settlement. But the story will never end. There will always be more clues and new ideas.

Below are two sets of dates for the earliest settlements in three places in Remote Oceania. These three places are very far from New Guinea. These are three of the last places that people settled. The people who made the settlements were Pacific Islanders. Again, scientists have changed their ideas about the dates. New clues seem to show that people did not arrive to the most distant places as early as some scientists thought.

**Table 1**

| Island | Previous estimate of settlement | New clues indicate earlier dates of settlement |
|---|---|---|
| Easter Island | 1600 years ago | 1100 years ago |
| New Zealand | 1700 years ago | 800 years ago |
| Hawaii | 2000 years ago | 1300 years ago |

## For you to try

- Look at Table 1. Find the islands on the regional map. Who lives there now? How do you think the first people got there?
- What do you think happened after people arrived in Remote Oceania?

## Human effects on new lands

Imagine stepping onto an island where no people had ever been. The birds might just look at you and not be afraid of you. You could walk up to them and take one away to cook (this is still possible on some islands). Many places must have had feasts at first. People did not have to think about recycling or reusing parts of the environment. Populations were very small. At first, settlers did not have to think about resource management.

Many of the remote islands of the Pacific are small. They have limited resources. Their history provides us with lessons on population growth and resource use.

Some islands must have been disappointments to the first settlers. Other islands started with strong settlements. Fish and food was there for everyone. Then populations grew and the resources could not grow as fast.

Remember Kritimati Island, Kiribati, the largest atoll in the world? Many seabirds nest there. The people who live on the island used to collect thousands of eggs. Now there are more people and fewer eggs. It is illegal to collect them. The birds are still not afraid of people because people have been there for less than a hundred years. There are clues that people came at least 700 years ago to Kritimati Island, but only stayed a couple of weeks each time to fish and eat birds.

Another famous example is Easter Island. First, remember the people in the northern islands of Papua New Guinea who made Lapita pottery about 4000 years ago. They started the migration and settlement of the Remote Pacific. One of the last places settled was Easter Island. No one is sure when people first arrived. Maybe it was as long as 1800 years ago or more recently. Maybe people have only been there for about 1100 years. Easter Island's area is about 170 square kilometres. The first people found some good resources, such as a good climate, fertile soils, animals and plants for food, and raw materials for clothing and building. The settlers brought resources with them to raise or grow on the island, such as fowl, bananas, sweet potatoes, taro and yams. The settlers also brought rats. These were a food source. But rats also ate resources themselves.

The first settlers feasted on the easily-caught birds and porpoises. These became rarer and more difficult to get as the population grew. Over time people had to adapt. They increased their agriculture.

Drying winds that took the moisture away from the soil is one problem the people faced. Like parts of Papua New Guinea, people used stones to prevent dry soil from blowing away. Sometimes they used stone mulches to hold moisture in the ground. Around Port Moresby, you can see some Motu gardeners using this same adaptation today.

## Population density at Easter Island

**Population density** is the number of people per square kilometre. Say the first settlers to Easter Island were a group of 20 people. The island is about 170 square kilometres, so the first population density would be 20 people divided by 170 or about 0.1 people per square kilometre. (The formula is: 20/170 = 0.1)

When the population grew to 200 people the density would be 200/170 or about 1.2 people per square kilometre. (The formula is: 200/170 = 1.17, which rounds to 1.2)

The population continued to grow. People adapted and intensified agriculture. They made many stone chicken houses and chicken runs. Maybe the population reached 30 000 people, maybe it only reached 15 000 people or maybe it just made 6000.

## For you to try

- Use the figures in the information in "Population density at Easter Island" to calculate the population density of the island.
- Discuss the following questions: How large could a population grow on 170 square kilometres? What resources are needed? What could people recycle or reuse?

The Easter Islanders divided into clans as the population grew. Clan chiefs had people make statues from the soft volcanic stone. Statues represented ancestors. The clans set completed statues on large platforms. The statues and platforms required many tonnes of rock. The rock had to be carved and moved. People used parts of trees to move the carved rock.

So people cut trees down for making agricultural land and for moving carved stone. Scientists have counted over 300 stone platforms and over 100 finished statues. For many years the statues presented a mystery. Europeans could not understand how they had been transported and erected. Now we know that many forest products were used to make ropes and wooden **transport systems**. Similar traditional transport systems have been used in Papua New Guinea on the coast. People used them to move newly made canoes from the forest to the sea.

This is one possible way that Easter Islanders may have transported the huge statues.

Between agriculture and statue making, all the forest was used up. There were too many people and not enough food. People started fighting and eating each other. Cannibalism and starvation reduced the population. People had chopped down all the forest and food trees. They had eaten all the land birds. Fighting continued for a long time. The clans knocked down each other's statues. The people stopped listening to the chieftains. Fight leaders took over until colonial times.

## For you to try

- Why didn't the people conserve their resources? Think of the reasons you might use to explain this.

Many people have wondered how the Easter Islanders lost all their forests. The island changed from rich forest to scrub and mainly grassland over 500 to 600 years. People have come up with some ideas to explain how this happened.

One idea is that there was a very important palm tree on Easter Island that provided valuable palm nuts for food, thatch for houses and timber for many items. This important resource became extinct. Some people have guessed that Islanders chopped down all their palm trees to move statues. Another explanation is that rats ate all the seeds, so no new palms could grow. Or perhaps clans chopped each other's palm trees down for payback. Or people were too busy fighting to care about palm seedlings.

The population grew so large that all the land was needed to grow crops. The soils became weak and were not replenished. Trees could not grow easily and people were too busy fighting for survival to worry about keeping their forest.

In other places, once people settled an area, they adapted and changed. They invented new ways to use the resources. The peoples of the Pacific Islands had many agricultural resources. They were good gardeners. They grew crops. In many places they also managed some forests like a big garden.

They also protected the resources of the coral reef. They made some places and some times taboo (tambu) for fishing or shell collection. The same was true for collecting birds and eggs in some places on land. Good managers with good resources survived well. Poor management in a difficult environment like Easter Island left many people to die.

A valley in Papua New Guinea.

The highland valleys of New Guinea, for example, show how people adapted to population pressure and deforestation. Scientists have found evidence of people planting casuarinas a long time ago in these highlands. The clues show that casuarinas were a major tree crop in the highland valleys of New Guinea 1 200 years ago. This covers both the Wahgi Valley in Papua New Guinea and the Baliem Valley in West Papua, Indonesia. Casurina tree crops appear in both places at about the same time.

### For you to try

- There were about a million people in the Papa New Guinea Highlands when Europeans finally first arrived about 80 years ago. Along with casuarinas, what other resource management ideas do you think the Highlanders used to sustain such a dense population?
- People used other trees as a resource. Write down the most important trees in your province. Explain how they are used as resources. Are any parts of them recycled or reused?

## Early European impacts and settlement

Europeans brought new settlement patterns to the Pacific. Eventually this resulted in a colonial period. Much of this you can explore in the next chapter on organisation. Cities, towns, plantations and mines are the biggest changes that European colonialism brought to **settlement patterns**.

The Europeans saw new resources in the Pacific. They took away minerals like gold and phosphate. The mining towns had good resources when the mines worked. The settlements often became poor when the mines closed. Both mines and plantations need people for labour. This has often changed settlement patterns and moved people to new places.

A mining town in Papua New Guinea.

In the worst cases, people became slaves. Blackbirders (people who kidnapped Pacific Islands people to use as slaves) raided Easter Island several times in the 1800s. The population was already down to about 3000 people in 1860. Blackbirders then took half of them to work and die in the guano (phosphate) mines of Peru.

Plantations often took good flat land. Coconut plantations spread across the Pacific followed by other crops like cacao, sugarcane, rubber and pineapples. Labour was imported when Pacific people would not work on plantations. This changed settlement patterns. The British brought Indian workers to Fiji for sugarcane plantations. Americans encouraged Japanese, Chinese and Philippinos to work on pineapple plantations in Hawaii. Blackbirders took Pacific Islanders, including Papua New Guineans, to work on sugarcane plantations in Queensland.

## For you to try

For your province, research the following and present your findings in class.

- Why have people settled in different places? Can you tell where settlement has traditionally been and what changes the colonial period made? Has there been new settlement since **Independence**?
- What types of settlement patterns does your province have and how are they different from other parts of Papua New Guinea?
- What do you think future settlements will be like in Papua New Guinea? Do you think your province will have more people over time? Do you think people will move to somewhere else?

## Population density now

When we look at settlement, we are looking at people. The total number of people is the population. The total population of Papua New Guinea is growing. In 2005 the population was growing at about 2.26 per cent each year. That means that for every 100 people in Papua New Guinea in 2005 there would be 102.6 in 2006. This means that for every thousand people in 2005, there would be 1026 in 2006.

The population chart shows how the population of Papua New Guinea will grow if the rate stays at 2.26 per cent each year. This is an estimate. It is using knowledge we have to make a good guess. The rate can change. It may be higher or lower. From 1980 to 1990 it was 2.4 per cent. If the rate becomes higher, this means that we will have more people sooner.

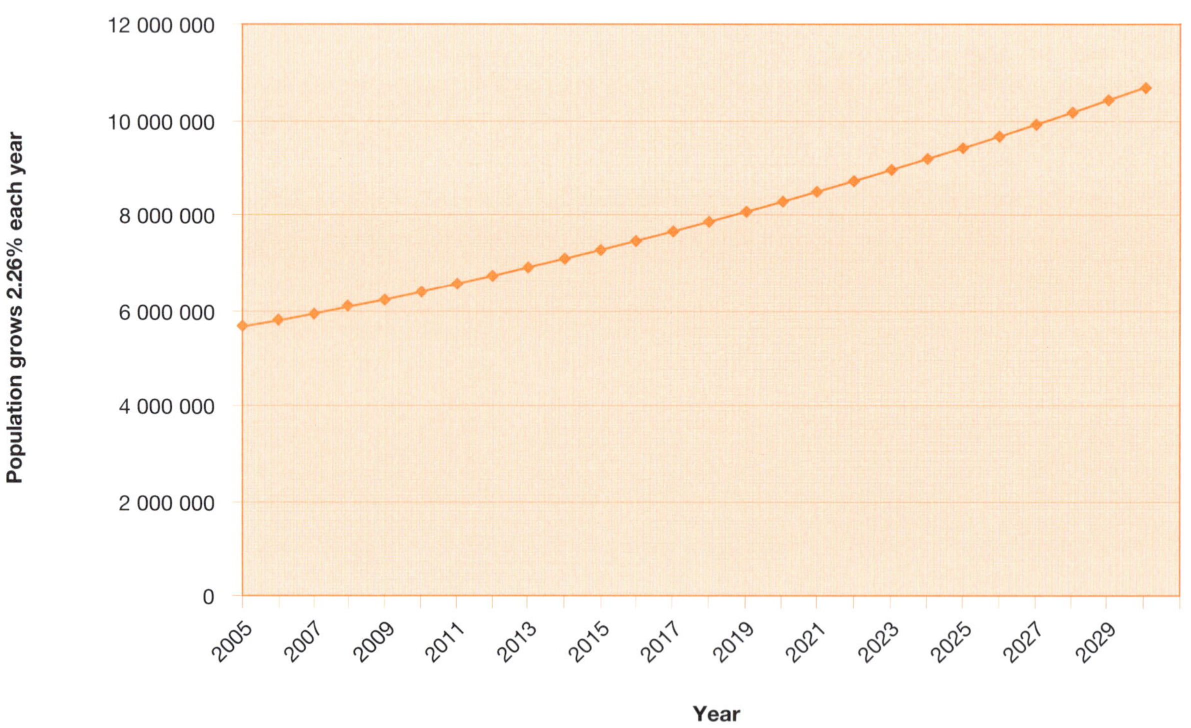

## For you to try

Study the chart *PNG Population Estimate* and answer the following questions.

- How old will you be when the population reaches eight million people? What about when it reaches 10 million people?
- What do you think will happen to settlement in your province as population grows?
- What do you think might lower population growth in your province? Will migration bring more or fewer people to your province?
- What other things could make the population grow faster or slower?

The average population density for all of Papua New Guinea is about eight people per square kilometre. This seems to tell us that there is a lot of land in Papua New Guinea. But in some parts of Papua New Guinea, there are few resources and a poor environment. This means that not many people will want to live in those places. In Western Province, for example, the lowlands are swampy and wet, and the mountains have a very high rainfall and poor soils. This means that it is not a place where people will want to settle. Life would be very difficult, so the population density is very low.

Population density is only 1 person per square kilometre in some remote parts of Papua New Guinea. On some small islands the density is over 500 people per square kilometre. Good agricultural land is under pressure in many places. There has been fighting in Southern Highlands Province as population density increases, but land to grow sweet potato stays the same.

Across the border, the Indonesian government has tried to settle people in parts of West Papua. People have come from the island of Java in Indonesia. The island of Java is smaller than Papua New Guinea, but it has rich volcanic soils. The population of Java is over 140 million people. Java has a very high population density but it has very fertile soils.

The Javanese who have come to West Papua have had many problems settling. The environment and resources are very different in New Guinea. Many have gone back to Java. Some have died of malaria. But people from other parts of the Indonesian archipelago have also come to West Papua. They have found it easier to adapt. Now about 40% of the people in West Papua are originally from another part of Indonesia.

Growing population density can be a big problem. Look at the map of Tarawa Atoll, Kiribati. This is one of the most densely populated parts of the Pacific Islands. There are over 30 000 people living on the atoll. The population growth rate is about 2.2% a year.

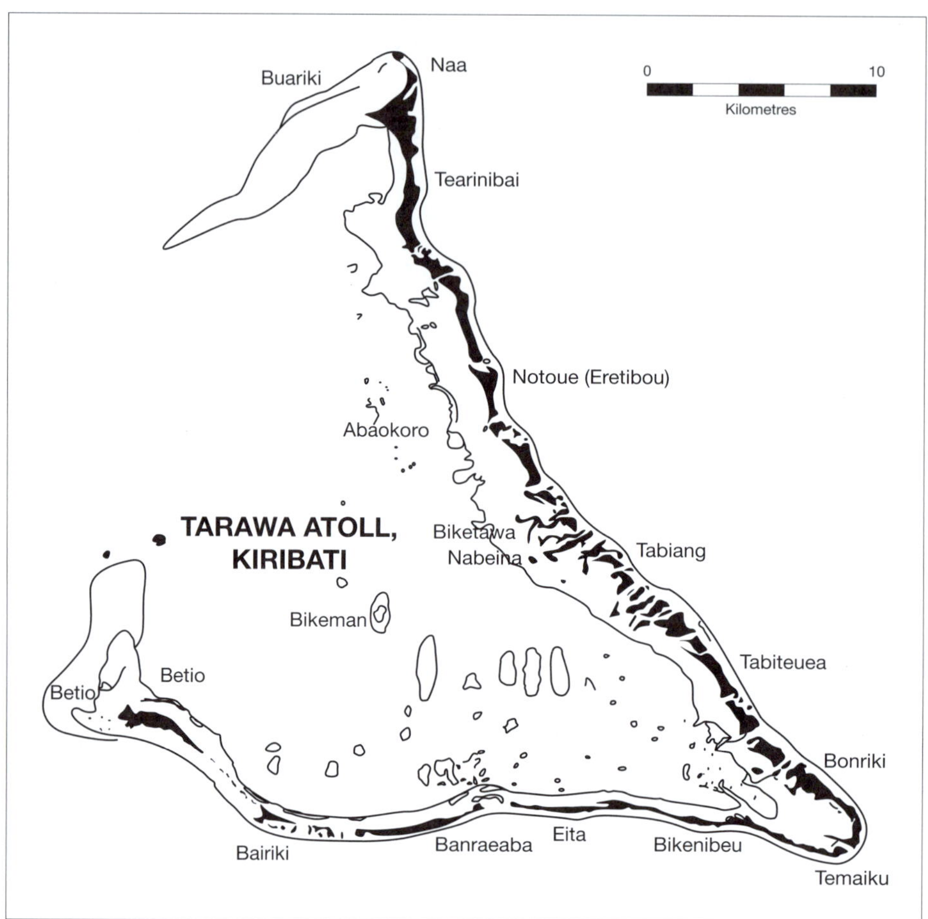


There are limited resources on Tarawa Atoll. The soil is poor, so is not good for food crops. Because there is so little land, even burying people is difficult. The people depend mainly on tuna fishing royalties, copra and international assistance for income. There is limited ground water and it is not well protected, so people must collect rainwater for safe drinking.

## For you to try

- Make an estimate of the square kilometres available for the population now and in ten years. The population density is around 1400 people per square kilometre.
- As a class, discuss what the people of Tarawa Atoll need to do to manage the resources and population.

Cities create resources for people. They provide cash income through jobs and business opportunities. They often have better schools and hospitals than are in rural areas. In the Pacific Islands, cities have attracted people. The population density around cities has grown. This can result in problems. A recent severe example is in the Solomon Islands.

Politics and race can lead to problems in urban areas. in 2006, a hotel burns in Honiara, the Solomon Islands capital.

Honiara, on the island of Guadalcanal, is the capital city of Solomon Islands. The population grew rapidly in Honiara and on Guadalcanal. Migrants from other islands came to the city. Many came from Malaita Island. The government had problems with corruption and managed badly. Traditional Guadalcanal land owners and Malaita migrants started to fight. The landowners were frightened that so many people were on their land. Fight leaders saw an opportunity to gain more resources.

## For you to try

- Research what has happened on Solomon Islands. What is the situation now?
- Can you find other examples of growing or shifting populations and disputes over resources? What can help and what are the solutions?

# NATURAL HAZARDS

A **natural hazard** is something that happens naturally that can harm human beings. A natural hazard can become a natural disaster when people are not prepared. This means that if people are prepared, a hazard does not have to become a disaster. However, sometimes it is too expensive or too difficult to prepare. In many places people have not been able to be prepared and so have learned to live with natural hazards.

There are many natural hazards in our region:

| | |
|---|---|
| avalanches and mud flows | cyclones |
| droughts | dust storms |
| earthquakes | fires |
| flooding | frost |
| rainstorms and rain damage | poisonous snakes |
| sharks | rapid sea level rise |
| tsunami | storm surges |
| windstorms and wind damage | volcanoes |

## For you to try

- Can you think of any other hazards to add to the list on this page? Now see what different groups you can divide the list into. What different groups can you think of? Discuss why you put hazards into these groups.
- What links can you find between hazards?
- What about crocodiles and wild pigs? Are these natural hazards or natural resources?
- Are mosquitoes and parasites another type of natural hazard? Think about the diseases they carry.

One way some people protect themselves from natural hazards is to buy insurance. For example, many people in Australia and New Zealand buy insurance to protect their homes or businesses against fire, flood and storm damage. Some urban people in places like Port Moresby or Suva in Fiji can insure their homes and businesses. In many rural parts of the Pacific, people do not have the money to buy this type of protection.

Storms cause hundreds of millions of dollars of damage every year in Australia. Tropical cyclones can cost even more in the damage they do. Most companies and many people are insured for storm damage in Australia. Big insurance companies have started to plan for more severe storms and floods.

Global warming, resulting from human activities, may cause more severe weather. Global warming may also result in more storms. The number of storms may increase. The strength of storms does now seem to be increasing. Insurance companies will have to pay more for more damage. People who cannot buy insurance will face higher risks.

### For you to try

- Divide the class into two groups. One group prepares a talk on who needs insurance for natural hazards, why they need it and who can afford it. The other group prepares a talk on who does not need insurance, other ways people can protect themselves from natural hazards without insurance, preventing loss before a natural hazard happens and recovering from losses without insurance after a natural hazard.

## Earthquakes

Most earthquakes that affect people happen around the edges of tectonic plates. Papua New Guinea and many of our neighbours are located on these edges (look at the picture of tectonic plates on page 14). Earthquakes are common and a major natural hazard.

Photograph courtesy of Tony Lolkes de Beer.

Sometimes engineers will say "Earthquakes do not kill people. It is falling buildings that kill." This means that you should build better buildings to withstand earthquakes. It can be expensive. It also requires special knowledge to make buildings strong for earthquakes. There also need to be laws to make builders do this. In many places, people are not well prepared for earthquakes.

### For you to try

- Consider the settlements in your province. These are the rural areas, towns and cities. How well prepared are they for earthquakes?

## Volcanoes

Volcanoes can be active, dormant or extinct. Active volcanoes are very dangerous because they release hot ash, gases and lava. Dormant volcanoes are "sleeping". This means that they might become active one day—maybe in 20 years or 100 or even 1000 more years. Extinct volcanoes are "dead", which means they cannot hurt anybody.

There are around 10 000 active or dormant volcanoes in the Pacific region alone. Papua New Guinea and many of its neighbours (such as the Solomon Islands, Hawaii, Indonesia and Vanuatu) have active volcanoes. Australia has dormant volcanoes.

Most volcanoes in the world are extinct. People thought that Mt Lamington in Oro Province, Papua New Guinea, was extinct until it exploded in 1951.

In 1994, two volcanoes around Rabaul erupted causing a great deal of damage.

The earthquake in Rabaul caused great damage.

# Tsunamis

Earthquakes at sea can also cause tsunamis. A major earthquake off the coast of Chile in South America triggered a tsunami that hit the Hawaiian Islands in 1960. The wave was over 10 metres high as it hit some parts of the islands and did several hundred million kinas of damage. After that, the Americans installed an early warning system to protect the people of Hawaii.

The earthquake that started the Asian tsunami of December 2004 struck the northern parts of Aceh in Indonesia almost immediately. Buildings fell down, trapping people. The earthquake was a warning that a tsunami would come shortly. Many people were trying to help trapped family members when the tsunami struck. This tsunami affected many other countries, such as Sri Lanka, Thailand, India, Kenya and Somalia. About 230 000 people were killed worldwide.

On 17 July 2006, another large tsunami hit the south coast of the island of Java, Indonesia. It killed over 600 people and damaged many buildings. This tsunami was caused by a powerful earthquake in the Indian Ocean. Some scientists think that there will be more earthquakes near Indonesia soon. The earthquakes will be a warning that another tsunami is coming.

## For you to try

- Imagine you are on the coast in Aceh when an earthquake strikes. Buildings fall down. People are calling for help. Some of your family are trapped. Discuss what you could do.
- How would you feel if you suspected a tsunami was coming soon? What would you do?

# Tropical storms and cyclones

Tropical storms and cyclones are hazards that many people in the tropical Pacific must live with. Tropical cyclones depend on a combination of wind and warm water to heat the air to start the storm system. The warmer the water becomes, the stronger the storm will be. The warm water can act like a fuel.

Cyclones passing over small island nations can cover them with water from storm surges. This happened to Tuvalu's main island in 1972 when Cyclone Bebe destroyed all the houses on Funafuti Atoll (the main island and capital of Tuvalu). One man went to the widest part of the island (the landing strip for international airplanes). The storm surge came straight across and he found himself swimming in water two metres deep.

Other storms have followed in Tuvalu, but none yet as severe as Cyclone Bebe. In the future there will be a worse storm, but no one is prepared for it now. The Tuvalu government has plans to develop a building code and sea walls at some vulnerable places.

Chuuk is a Micronesian island country. It used to be called Truk. On 1 July, 2002, Tropical Cyclone Chataan struck Chuuk. In four hours, 50 centimetres of rain fell on parts of Chuuk. That is half a metre of water. Along with high surfs and flooding, there were more than 30 landslides. Many people were caught completely by surprise and were unprepared for the disaster.

Forty-eight people died and many were injured. Hundreds of buildings were destroyed, leaving 2000 people homeless. Because there was no drainage system in some towns, the sewage system backed up. There was also no clean drinking water. These circumstances made waterborne diseases (such as cholera and diarrhoea) a real threat.

## For you to try

- What kinds of problems do cyclones cause for small islands in the Pacific?
- How do you think people could prepare for a cyclone?

# The good part of natural hazards

Natural hazards are not all bad. They can actually create resources and build islands. For example, the surge and storm waves from Cyclone Bebe in 1972 at Funafuti Atoll built a permanent rubble rampart from broken coral. The rampart measured 3.5 metres high, 37 metres wide and 18 km long. Similar coral rubble ramparts have been created by storms on other islands, such as on Kiritimati Island, Kiribati. Floods also replenish soils.

One of the reasons why people settle near volcanoes is that the soil is so rich and fertile. For many people, the risks of volcanoes are not as important as the benefits of good soil and large crops. Volcanoes in Indonesia, Fiji, New Zealand, Hawaii, Papua New Guinea and New Caledonia have helped create fertile soils. In some cases, they have replenished the soils (and continue to replenish the soils). Easter Island's volcano is extinct, and part of the island's problem has been soil depletion.

## For you to try

- Are there any natural hazards (such as volcanoes and storms) that have been good for your province? List these hazards and their benefits.

# 2

# Organisation

## Chapter summary

In this chapter you will have the opportunity to:

✓ look at different governments in the Pacific Islands

✓ compare economic and social development in selected Pacific Islands

✓ identify ways that you might contribute to national and regional development.

## Syllabus references

Strand: Organisation

Sub-strand: Provincial, national and regional social and economic organisation

Outcomes

**7.2.1** Students are able to identify the main government features for provinces, the nation and the region

**7.2.2** Students are able to describe provincial, national and regional development

**7.2.3** Students are able to contribute to the social and economic development of the province, nation and neighbouring regions.

# Government

## What is government?

Government is the way in which people are ruled. Governments can be ruled by one person (like a king), by a small group of people (like an important family) or by all the people. When a country is ruled by all the people, the people elect representatives who will speak for them rather than just for themselves.

Governments make and use rules. Traditional rules can be spoken and handed down from one generation to another. Examples are rules for big men and traditional chiefs. Some of these rules have lasted for hundreds or even thousands of years. They were never written down.

Formal governments in Papua New Guinea now write the rules down. These are laws and policies. Laws and policies are made by the national and provincial governments. The laws are based on the **constitution** of Papua New Guinea. The constitution is the document that provides the base for governing the nation.

National Parliament at Waigani

In Papua New Guinea, the government provides services such as schools, health centres, the police and the military. The government collects money to pay for these services. The government gets money from taxes and charges. Most people in Papua New Guinea pay some goods and services tax. Government also gets more money from the big companies in mining, fisheries, forestry and agriculture.

Government also makes plans and rules for developing Papua New Guinea and supporting the people. Papua New Guinea has three formal levels of government:

- Local Government
- Provincial Government
- National Government

## For you to try

- Think about the three levels of government. Then discuss each of them. What do they do for you and your family? What are they doing for your community?

The government of Papua New Guinea and many of its neighbours also get assistance from other countries. This is called **development assistance**. This assistance can be money, people or things that people need. Australia and New Zealand assist Papua New Guinea and other smaller Pacific Islands with many different types of assistance. Japan and the European Union are two other donors. We call assistance between governments *bilateral aid*.

# Government in Papua New Guinea

Papua New Guinea is a **democracy**. This is a special type of government. A democratic government is ruled by the people. In a democracy the people elect their representatives. People elect the government to serve them.

In Papua New Guinea, the Prime Minister is the Head of Government (the Queen is the Head of State). A Deputy Prime Minister works with the Prime Minister and can substitute for him when needed. The national government of Papua New Guinea has many areas for serving the people. Many of these areas come under ministries. Here is a list of major ministries:

| | | |
|---|---|---|
| Agriculture and Livestock | Correctional Services | Culture and Tourism |
| Defense | Education | Environment and Conservation |
| Finance | Fisheries | Foreign Affairs and Immigration |
| Forestry | Health | Housing |
| Inter-Government Relations | Justice | Labour and Employment |
| Lands and Physical Planning | Mining | Petroleum and Energy |
| Public Service | Treasury | Social Welfare & Development |
| Trade and Industry | Transport and Aviation | |

## For you to try

- Look at the list of different ministries. Which ones do you know about? What services do they provide? Investigate two of the ministries that you do not know about and find out the services they provide to the people of Papua New Guinea.

People elect parliamentarians to represent them at the national level. We have national **elections** every five years. Politicians ask people for their votes at these elections. The politicians make many promises. If the promises are broken, people do not vote for those politicians in the next election. Since Independence, most Papua New Guinea politicians have only been elected once.

## What people make up the government?

The government is made up of different people: **elected officials**, **public servants** and appointed individuals.

The elected officials are the representatives chosen by the people. These are the Parliamentarians at the national level. They come from many different political parties. Different parties must come together after the election. They should form a majority to govern.

Every five years after the election, a Prime Minister and Cabinet members are selected. There is only one Prime Minister but Cabinet numbers can change. The different political parties in the government will want as many Cabinet seats as they can get.

Public servants are another set of people in government. They carry out the plans and policies of the elected government. Public servants are not elected. They are hired for their skills. Part of their contract is to serve the government and the people.

Parliament appoints judges to serve the justice system. Judges are constitutional officials who cannot be removed easily once they are appointed. Judges are covered by the constitution or statutes. This gives them security of having their job until retirement or a major breach of their duties. It means that judges should not be easy to influence.

The Ombudsman is another example of a constitutional official. Anyone can complain to the Ombudsman about a problem with a government department. Also, the Ombudsman investigates complaints about leadership code violations. This is when a leader is accused of corruption. The position of Ombudsman is protected by the constitution. Like a judge, it is hard to dismiss an Ombudsman without very good reasons.

## Traditional governments

For thousands of years, Papua New Guinea had traditional governments. These were very small. Each group could have their own government. The leaders were usually big men in charge of extended families and clans. There were big women who had special knowledge, such sanguma meri. There were chieftains in a few places. The Mekeo and Trobriand Islanders have a system of chiefs who are born into leadership positions.

Most of Papua New Guinea did not have leaders by birth. Each generation had new leaders. For the big man, it does not matter who their father or mother was. What is important is what they are able to do.

Two types of traditional government are common in the Pacific Islands. There is the big man system in most of New Guinea, Vanuatu, Solomon Islands and parts of Fiji. Chieftain systems existed on other Pacific Islands. The largest chiefdom systems were in Tonga, New Zealand and Hawaii.

The Hawaiian islands developed complex agricultural systems. The traditional Hawaiian farmers produced taro, sweet potato, sugar cane, banana and gourds. They also used fish ponds to produce milkfish and mullet. The systems allowed them to produce large surpluses. The extra food meant that some people did not have to work in the gardens. Some scientists think that producing surplus food resulted in the chiefdom system.

The traditional Hawaiian system had different levels of chiefs. The top chief or king had other lesser chiefs. The chiefs were supported by traditional religious men and by warriors. These people were supported by farmers. Warriors could spend some time in gardens and farmers could fight.

Big man: yesterday and today

## For you to try

- Look at the drawing *Big man: yesterday and today*. What ideas can you add to the drawing? What makes the big men in your province big men?
- Can you name some big women? Why are there so few women in Parliament?
- Make a drawing titled: *Big woman: yesterday and today*.
- Discuss the traditional governments of your province. Think about other provinces in Papua New Guinea. Did people have complex agricultural systems? Did they produce a surplus? Did a chieftain system start?

## A settlement disappears in the Pacific Islands

A few Pacific island settlements completely disappeared before Europeans came. One of these settlements was on Henderson Island in the southeast Pacific.

Henderson is the largest island of the Pitcairn group of islands. It is an elevated limestone island. People settled on Henderson island round 1200 years ago. People lived there for about 650 years. They made mumus, brought trade goods like pearl shell and obsidian to the island. They traded with people on Pitcairn and Mangareva islands. But about 550 years ago, all the people were gone. Why?

### Clues

- Traditional Polynesian crops cannot grow on Henderson Island and wood is scarce.
- Henderson Island had turtles, parrots with red feathers and fruit doves with red feathers.
- Henderson Islanders traded turtle meat and the red feathers with the people of Pitcairn island, who had mumu stones and obsidian.
- Henderson Islanders traded with Mangareva Islanders for wood for making canoes and pearl shells for making fish hooks and other tools.
- The Mangareva people used up their forest. They had no more trees.
- All the fruit doves and the all the parrots vanished on Henderson Island. Four other types of bird on the island also became extinct. (Maybe the people ate them. Maybe the birds could not live without the forest. Maybe people killed all the red-feathered birds for trade.)
- The last Polynesian settlers on Henderson Island used local shells for tools. The local shells made very weak tools.

That's the first parrot I've seen for a long, long time. Where have they all gone?

What will we do without them? How will we survive?

## For you to try

Read the clues about Henderson Island then do the following activities.

- Draw your own pictures of your story about what finally happened to the Henderson Island people.
- Read the clues. Discuss whether the traditional government failed the people of Henderson Island. Did something else happen?

Most traditional governments in the Pacific islands lasted for a long time. People fought over resources, so some groups became weaker or stronger. Some places were expanding their territories when Europeans started colonising the Pacific Islands. The Kingdom of Tonga was expanding into Samoa, for example. Groups were expanding and contracting in many parts of Papua New Guinea. Europeans stopped these processes. Boundaries that had been fluid became frozen.

# Colonial government

Papua New Guinea and most of its neighbours have been colonies. Papua New Guinea was only a **colony** for a short time (although the first colonial claims started nearly 500 years ago). Some of its neighbours were colonies for longer. Europeans occupied and colonised parts of Indonesia, all of Australia and New Zealand long before Papua New Guinea and many other Pacific Islands were colonised.

The Spanish and Portuguese were the first Europeans to come to Asia and to some of the Pacific Islands. They wanted gold and spices. They started explorations in the 1500s. They found very little in Oceania. They focused on Asia and the Americas where they found plenty of gold, spices and other resources.

## The Dutch in Indonesia

The Netherlands is a small country in Europe. The people in the Netherlands are called Dutch. The Netherlands became an important European trading nation in the 1600s. They followed the Spanish and Portuguese to Asia and the Pacific. The Dutch fought with the Spanish and Portuguese, and took away some of their colonies.

The Dutch started colonies in Indonesia around 1645. They stayed in parts of Indonesia for over 300 years. The Indonesians had to fight the Dutch from 1945 to 1949 before they finally became independent. Indonesians had to fight very hard for independence. The Dutch burned down whole villages and many civilians were killed.

Indonesia took over West Papua in 1964 and made the Dutch leave. Indonesia now has a democracy. It is new because the military ran Indonesia from 1965 to 2000. The national parliament of Indonesia meets in Jakarta, its capital. Each province also has a democratically elected government. The national government is trying to decentralise and strengthen local governments. There are over 400 of these local governments.

A political rally in the new democracy at the Indonesian Independence Monument (*photo courtesy of Aji Indrarto*)

## For you to try

- Find out about Indonesia and its government. Compare what you find with government in Papua New Guinea. What is the same? What is different?

## República Democrática de Timor-L'Este (East Timor)

The nation of Timor L'Este was a colony of Portugal for nearly 400 years. During all that time there were fights for independence. Finally, in 1975, Portugal decided that Timor L'Este could be free. That same year, the Indonesian government invaded. The Indonesian military government made Timor L'Este an Indonesian colony for another 25 years. Timor L'Este is now an independent country with a parliamentary democracy like Papua New Guinea. Timor L'Este gained independence on 20 May, 2002.

## The British claim Australia

The Aboriginal peoples of Australia ran their own small traditional governments for at least 50 000 years. They had a deep attachment to the land and many different systems to manage resources. Despite this, the British declared they owned the whole island continent and all its resources. They recognised no Aboriginal ownership.

The first permanent European settlement in Australia was at Sydney. It started as a place for British convicts—a prison settlement. The Aboriginal people had many disputes with the settlers. They saw them take fish from the harbour and shoot kangaroos in the bush. The settlers did not share any of this with the Aboriginal people. They did not understand about sharing what they took from the land and sea. This led to the first fights.

Australia and New Zealand both started as British colonies. Britain started a colony in Australia in 1786. The Commonwealth of Australia started in 1901 when it became a constitutional democracy. Like Papua New Guinea, the Queen of England is still the Head of State for Australia.

## Colonial Government in New Guinea

In the 1500s, both Spain and Portugal made claims to own New Guinea. Malay traders were visiting the north coast of West Papua before the first Europeans. Maybe they also made some claims to trading rights. Malay traders gave the name Papua to the people. It means "frizzy-haired". Ynigo Ortiz, a Spanish explorer, gave the name Nueva Guinea (New Guinea) to the island in 1545. After the Spanish and Portuguese, many other countries laid claim to the island.

The British, Dutch and Germans were the successful colonisers of New Guinea. The colony of Queensland, Australia, tried to make Papua a colony in 1884 to prevent the Germans from colonising Papua. But Great Britain said that a colony could not have its own colony. Instead, Great Britain made Papua a protectorate in 1885 to keep the Germans out. Great Britain gave the colony of Papua to Australia when Australia became an independent Commonwealth in 1901.

The British raised the Union Jack (the British flag) over Port Moresby in 1884 when they claimed the south-eastern part of the country as their own.

The Dutch did very little to their half of New Guinea. They made other people in Indonesia work very hard. For 50 years (1830–1870) people in Java had to grow a part of their crops or work part of the year for no money. The Dutch left the people of West Papua alone because there were no easy resources to take. The Dutch agreed to give independence to Indonesia in 1949, but they kept West Papua. Indonesia then claimed and took West Papua from the Dutch in 1963.

## For you to try

- Most countries recognise West Papua as part of Indonesia. Vanuatu is one country that openly supports independence for West Papua. Discuss the advantages and disadvantages for West Papuans being Indonesians.

A German colonist in German New Guinea in the early 1900s.

Papua and German New Guinea were divided between the Australians and Germans until 1914. The Europeans then fought World War I. Germany lost the war and lost all its colonies. Australian soldiers looked after New Guinea from 1914 until 1921. The League of Nations then asked Australia to govern New Guinea. The laws and conditions were different in Papua and New Guinea even though Australia was in charge of both places.

Papua was a colony. New Guinea was a protectorate. The names were different but the situation was similar. Papua New Guinea people were ruled by others.

## Colonial Pacific Islands

Most small Pacific islands had become formal colonies by 1900. For example, Chile claimed Easter Island in 1888. Germany and the USA claimed Samoa and divided it for themselves in the 1890s, and The King of Tonga had to sign a Treaty of Friendship with Britain in 1900, which placed a British Resident in the King's cabinet to give advice.

The end of World War I in 1918 started many colonial changes. Germany was pushed out of the Pacific and lost all its Pacific colonies. In the 1920s, the Japanese took over all the German colonies north of the equator. Britain, Australia and New Zealand took the German colonies south of the equator. Very few island people saw many benefits. Good jobs and profits all went to the colonisers.

The Japanese controlled a great deal of Papua New Guinea during World War II.

World War II was fought in the Pacific from 1941 to 1945. Again the fighting brought many changes. Japanese military forces invaded deep into New Guinea and the Solomon Islands to the south, and into Kiribati to the east. In some places, Pacific islanders suffered under the Japanese. For example, the Japanese forced many people from Nauru to go to Chuuk as labourers. But Indonesian and other Asian people suffered even more. At just one mine on the island of Sulawesi in Indonesia, the Japanese military worked 4000 Indonesians to death.

The Japanese military became harsher when the Japanese forces starting losing World War II. Islanders suffered, but again, Asians suffered more. The Japanese left 5000 of their Indian helpers to die of starvation in the Sepik.

France has kept all its colonies since World War II. The USA has kept some colonies and entered into pacts of free association with others. But many Pacific Island countries gained independence. British, New Zealand and Australian colonies started becoming independent with Samoa first in 1962.

| Table 2: Some Pacific Island colonies that have gained independence | | |
|---|---|---|
| **Colony** | **Coloniser (year colonised)** | **Independence** |
| Samoa | Split by Germany and USA (1892)<br>New Zealand takes western part after WWII | 1962 |
| Vanuatu | France (1768), Britain (1774)<br>(held jointly until independence) | 1980 |
| Fiji | Great Britain (1874) | 1970 |
| Kiribati | Great Britain (1892) | 1970 |
| Solomon Islands | Spain, then Britain (1892) | 1978 |

| Table 3: Some Pacific Island colonies that have not gained independence | | |
|---|---|---|
| **Colony** | **Coloniser (year colonised)** | **Status** |
| New Caledonia | Annexed by France (1853) | Territory of France |
| French Polynesia | France (1843) | Territory of France |
| Hawaii | USA (1898) | Became state of USA 1959 |
| Guam | Spain (1521), USA (1898),<br>Japan (1941), USA (1944) | Territory of the USA |

## For you to try

- Look at Table 2. On the regional map, locate the countries that have gained independence. See what news you can find out about them now. How well are their governments doing?
- Look at Table 3. On the regional map, locate the countries that have not gained independence. In groups, discuss why they are still part of another country.

## Independence still a question for some

Tokelau is a small territory that has been administered by New Zealand since 1926. It was claimed by Britain in 1889. The total population is around 1500 people. The territory consists of three small atolls. You can find it on the map between New Zealand and Hawaii. It is in the middle between these two places.

In February of 2006, the people of Tokelau voted on their future status. The government of New Zealand arranged a referendum designed to give the Tokelauans self-government. It would be the world's smallest self-governing **state**. But the people voted against self-government. They prefer the New Zealand administration. While people in Tokelau are happy to stay with New Zealand, groups have been fighting for many years in West Papua and New Caledonia to become independent states.

This unofficial flag of Tokelau has been used since 1989.

The Organisasi Papua Merdeka (OPM), or Free Papua Movement, is no longer as active as in the 1970s and1980s but still has support in West Papua. The Front Liberation Nationale Kanak et Socialiste (FLNKS), or Kanak and Socialist National Liberation Front, has fought French colonists and military in New Caledonia. Like the OPM, it has been less active in recent years. Protest groups supporting native pride and traditions are active in Hawaii and Tahiti and New Zealand.

### For you to try

- Divide the class and hold a debate about the advantages and disadvantages for people being a colony or being independent. One side can argue the case for staying a colony like New Caledonia, Tokelau, French Polynesia, West Papua and Hawaii. The other side can argue for the advantages of independence for countries like the Solomon Islands, Vanuatu, Fiji and Papua New Guinea.

## The nuclear Pacific

Nuclear weapons have been tested in the Pacific. Colonial powers used the Pacific for these tests because it was remote and distant from their own lands. The United States of America's most famous tests were on Bikini Atoll in the Marshall Islands from 1946 to 1958. It is still not safe for the people to return there. Britain tested nuclear weapons in the early 1950s in a desert site in South Australia.

Later, Britain and the USA tested nuclear weapons at Christmas Island in the 1950s and early 1960s. The tests were some 9- to 10-thousand metres in the air above the atoll. Birds were blinded and killed but no permanent damage was done to the atoll. After the tests, Britain gave the island to Kiribati. Many people have been upset by the testing. The last colonial power to conduct tests in the Pacific was France.

**Table 4: Nuclear testing by colonial governments**

| Place | Country | Number of tests |
|---|---|---|
| Johnston Island (Part of the Line Islands) | USA | 12 |
| Christmas Island (Part of the Line Islands) | Britain and USA | 30 |
| Malden Island (Part of the Line Islands) | USA | 3 |
| Fangataufa Atoll | France | 12 |
| Mururoa Atoll | France | 179 |
| Marshall Islands | USA | 66 |
| Muralinga, Australia | Britain | 12 |

### For you to try

- Look at Table 4 and find the places on a map. Debate whether these places are so small and or far away that it did not really matter if they were used for nuclear testing.

There have been over 2000 nuclear tests since 1945. In 1963, the Limited Test Ban Treaty was signed by the United States and the Soviet Union to stop nuclear testing in the atmosphere, in outer space and underwater. Other tests continued underground. France kept testing in the Pacific until February 1996. In 1996, the United Nations General Assembly voted to adopt the Comprehensive Nuclear Test Ban Treaty to stop all nuclear testing. France, Britain and the USA have all signed this treaty, along with many more countries. A few countries are still testing nuclear weapons, but not in the Pacific.

France has released very little information about Mururoa Atoll testing, which only stopped in 1996. The Americans also assured Bikini Islanders that they could go back to their atoll sometime after the tests. The islanders tried once but it has never been safe enough. Similarly the British and Australian governments assured people that tests at Muralinga were safe. Reports and tests have shown this was not true. All the governments that tested nuclear weapons in the Pacific claimed that they were safe.

## French "lied" to Pacific on N-tests

France lied to the people of French Polynesia about the effects of radioactive fallout from nuclear tests carried out on their islands more than 30 years ago, according to an investigative report issued yesterday by the French territory's assembly ...

It says classified defence information from 1965–1967 shows France lied to the local population in saying the open-air tests would not affect them ...

The inquiry also found that French scientists failed to predict that winds would blow fallout from the giant mushroom cloud to neighbouring inhabited atolls.

The committee said that France's defence ministry tried to subvert its six-month investigation by refusing its members access to government documents as well as to test sites that remain under army control.

*The Canberra Times*,
Saturday, February 11, 2006

### For you to try

Read the article on the French nuclear tests.

- How long has the information been kept before release?
- Many people asked, "If these tests are so safe, why do you have to do them out here?" What do you think the answer is? What about other nuclear tests?

# States and nations: Papua New Guinea and the region

## What is a state?

Is a state different from a nation? There are many ways to define a state. A **sovereign** state is a free country. It has a physical territory that it controls and governs. The sovereign state is an organisation administered with rules and laws. Citizens and all others in the state are subject to its rules. This is the legal system. So we can call it an administrative legal structure.

A nation can be a state, but a sovereign state is not always a nation. A nation has a national identity. The people of a nation feel or believe that they all share some part of a common **culture**, history or heritage. The people of a nation feel that they are united by some shared experience.

### For you to try

Divide the class into groups and have each group discuss one of the following. Each group will then report back to the class.

- What common experiences help bring Papua New Guineans together?
- Is Papua New Guinea a nation or is it becoming a nation?

Independence has not been easy for many small island states. We can use the terms *emerging state*, *fragile state* and *failed state* to describe these states. All the recently independent states of the Pacific can be called emerging states. Some, such as the Solomon Islands and Nauru, have very serious problems. They are now called fragile states.

The fighting that erupted in the Solomon Islands was reducing it to a failed state. No one had control. Fight leaders were torturing and killing people. Australia sent a military force to establish order and assist the formation of a new government. The Solomon Islands may remain a fragile state for a long time. Will new governments be able to do better than the old ones? Or will they slip back to corruption and violence when the Australian presence is gone?

Nauru was one of the richest independent island countries in the Pacific. The island had been mined for phosphate when it was a colony. Britain and Australia agreed to pay millions of dollars in compensation for the mining. Bad government management and corruption lost all the money. The island became bankrupt. That means the government does not have the money to provide services. The question is, how long will it take Nauru to become stronger … or will it be a failed state?

## Traditional *versus* modern systems

The traditional systems of chiefs and kings have been in conflict against modern democracy. Samoa, Fiji and Tonga are examples of states that are between the two systems.

The traditional Samoan system of government is the matai system of chiefs. The matai have power and influence as chiefs. They had special voting powers until 1990. Since 1990 there has been universal suffrage in Samoa. That means that all adults can vote in elections.

A Samoan matai has a great deal of power.

Traditionally, the chiefs in the Samoan matai system were very powerful. In the 1980s a matai chief shot a villager who disobeyed him. The chief argued that he had the power to kill if disobeyed. The court disagreed. The state was setting limits.

Fiji has had much more serious power struggles. There have been **coups** starting in 1987. The traditional chiefs of eastern Fiji have fought for their traditional powers. They have been fighting against Fijians from the west, who have a traditional big-man system, and the Indian Fijians who came during colonial times. The coups have hurt the Fiji economy. Fiji now has a new constitution that discriminates against Indian Fijians. The deeper problem is between eastern and western Fijians. Will the eastern chieftain system be able to adapt and accept democratic government?

Tonga has been settled for about 3600 years. In 2005, it was one of the last true monarchies on earth. The king was very powerful. The king's children (princes and princesses) have been taking many resources. This makes a weak economy and gives little chance to people who are not royals.

King George Tupou V of Tonga

Many Tongans would now like a more democratic type of government. Protestors burned down a house belonging to a prince in late 2005. In 2006, small changes started to appear at the top levels of government, and there was much more burning and riots. Tonga may be moving towards more democracy or towards instability. You will have to research the answers.

# Resources in the Pacific region

All countries can divide their resources into two kinds: renewable and non-renewable. Renewable resources are resources that we will not run out of if we take care of them properly and do not use them all up. These resources include things like vegetation (trees and other plants) and animals. Plants and animals can reproduce, so if we take care of them and use them well, we will not run out of them.

Non-renewable resources are things like gold, phosphate and petroleum. These things cannot reproduce they way that animals and plants can, so once they are gone they are gone forever.

## For you to try

- Divide into groups and make lists of all the renewable and non-renewable resources you think are in Papua New Guinea and other Pacific Islands. Compare your lists and decide which resources are the most valuable.

# Blackbirding

When Europeans first arrived in the Pacific they saw many resources that they wanted for themselves. There was gold, copra, and land for sugar and coffee. But there were also human beings, which many Europeans thought of as just something else that could be bought, stolen or sold. Consequently, human beings were some of the first resources taken from the Pacific Islands and some other island neighbours of Papua New Guinea.

The Portuguese took slaves and sandalwood from East Timor for over 300 years. They started about 1550 and most sandalwood was gone by 1850 but slavery continued after that. In 1847 an Australian named Benjamin Boyd brought the first indentured labourers from the Pacific Islands to Australia. He brought 65 Ni-Vanuatuans to work in the sugar and cotton fields. This was the start of the blackbird trade.

"Blackbirding" is the name given to taking people as indentured servants, usually by tricking them or kidnapping. It was not considered true slavery as people were paid and were officially "free". But, of course, they were not. They were not free to go home or to find other employment until their term of service was over. This practice was outlawed in 1904 because it was considered very much like slavery. By that time, 65 000 Pacific Islanders had been brought to Australia to work in the sugarcane fields of Queensland.

Blackbirding started a trade in weapons. Pistols and rifles were traded to Pacific Islanders. Modern small arms are another type of resource and continue to be a problem. They have been used in conflicts in Bougainville, the Solomon Islands and the Highlands as well as by criminals.

## Renewable resources from the Pacific

Many of the Pacific Islands have similar agricultural and other renewable resources. Some of the agricultural resources are no longer produced in some places. It has become too expensive to produce them. Other places can produce them for less.

Table 5 shows some of the major resources (including those that are declining) in the region.

**Table 5: Some island resources**

| Countries | Resources | Status |
|---|---|---|
| Hawaii and Fiji | Copra | • stopped in Hawaii<br>• minor industry in Fiji<br>• still important in many other Pacific Islands |
| Hawaii and Fiji | Sugar | • stopped in Hawaii<br>• major industry in Fiji |
| Hawaii, Fiji and Vanuatu | Coffee | • minor industry in Hawaii<br>• stopped in Fiji<br>• growing industry in Vanuatu |
| Hawaii, Fiji, Cook Islands, Samoa | Fruit | • a major industry that is now a declining industry in Hawaii<br>• a minor industry in Fiji, Samoa and Cook Islands (exports to New Zealand) |
| Tonga and Vanuatu | Vanilla | • declining rapidly in Tonga<br>• a minor industry in Vanuatu |
| Solomon Islands and Fiji | Timber | • an important industry but badly managed in the Solomon Islands<br>• disputes over forest resources in Fiji are one cause of some coups and political problems |
| Solomon Islands, Tonga, Samoa and Kiribati | Fish | • fishing, fish processing and tuna fishing royalties are important for all these countries<br>• tuna stocks in general are getting smaller. |

## For you to try

Look at Table 5. Divide the class into groups to discuss, research and report on one or two of the following:

- How similar are these renewable resources to those that Papua New Guinea produces?
- Can you find examples where other uses for land can produce better profits?
- How **sustainable** are these products? What other resources are needed to produce them? How well protected are these renewable resources?
- Research another renewable resource that is or was produced in the Pacific Islands and Papua New Guinea, and report on its present situation and future. (A few examples are chillies, cocoa, fibres, rubber, oil palm, pearls, pearl shell, trepang and whaling.)

## Non-renewable resources

Non-renewable resources are resources that are taken away (extracted). Mining is an example of an extractive industry. Once minerals, such as gold and phosphate, are removed from the ground, we have no way of replacing them.

Phosphate comes from bird droppings (guano). Birds nested on some Pacific Islands for many thousands of years. Their guano built up and hardened over time. The guano turned into a type of rock that we call phosphate, which is an important fertiliser. For example, the dairy farmers of New Zealand and the wheat farmers of Australia used Pacific Island phosphate for a long time.

Banaba and Nauru are two important islands where phosphate was mined. Banaba Island is also called Ocean Island. It is now part of Kiribati. Banaba Island did not have very many resources for the islanders. The soil was poor and there was little fresh water. There were few places to grow crops. Still, people had survived and adapted. In 1900 phosphate mining began. There were about 2400 Banabans at the time of first European contact. By 1914 there were only 400 Banabans left. Today the mining is finished. There is very little development to show for it. The miners have left and the population is decreasing as people go to other places for work and income.

Phosphate mining in Nauru.

The Germans made Nauru a protectorate in 1888. The Nauruans had some good gardening land and reasonable water supplies. Their population declined with European contact and almost all the traditional culture was lost. The British had the mining lease on Nauru. They started mining in 1906. They used Japanese and other indentured or contract labour. They paid rents to the Nauru people. Britain, Australia and New Zealand administered Nauru after World War I. There were about 1800 Nauruans at the start of World War II. The Japanese occupiers sent 1200 Nauruans to Chuuk. Only 737 survived. Nauru gained independence in 1967. It received hundreds of millions of dollars from Britain and Australia for mining damage to the island.

## For you to try

- Find more information about Nauru or Banaba (Ocean) Island. Banaba is very small so it will be harder to find news about it. Divide the class into four groups to debate whether Banaba and Nauru would have been better off with no guano.

Spanish explorers along the coast of Papua New Guinea reported finding traces of gold in 1528. Another 350 years passed before gold mining started in Papua New Guinea. People protected their resources. The first gold mines came in the 1870s at Misima and Woodlark Islands.

Major gold mining on the mainland started in the 1920s at Bulolo and Wau, which became important towns in the 1930s. They had with some of the highest air transport in the world. The airplanes were put in place to serve the mines.

But dredging machinery used for gold extraction tore the land up. Millions of dollars worth of gold was taken from the land, while land for farming and the habitats of many animals were destroyed. Once the mining companies were finished taking the gold, they did nothing to restore the land to what it once was. No trees were planted and the land was not restored so that it could be used for farming or other uses. Originally, the people of Bulolo and Wau did not know that they could demand compensation for their destroyed land. Politicians and activists are still trying to get money from the mining companies to help restore the land and make it useful again.

## For you to try

- How different is the Wau and Bulolo mining story from Banaba and Nauru Islands?
- What type of air services do Wau and Bulolo have today? What is left there from the mining?

Today minerals are still very important for Papua New Guinea. Gold and copper are two major exports. Mines are working at Lihir, Ok Tedi, Misima, Porgera and in other provinces. Fiji has been a smaller gold producer with amounts declining over time.

The Panguna Copper Mine in Bougainville was a very important resource for Papua New Guinea. The mine produced 45 per cent of Papua New Guinea's export earnings. Almost half the nation's export earnings came from Panguna, starting from Independence until the mine was closed in 1990.

Some people of Bougainville had wanted their own independence even before Papua New Guinea became independent in 1975. They argued that the mine royalties should all go to them. Instead, Bougainville became a province. Because of Bougainville, all provinces were given more responsibilities and a larger share of royalties for resources. All provinces became a little more independent. All of them were still part of the nation.

Toward the end of the 1980s some local people started fighting the Panguna mine. A rebellion followed. Fighting lasted for many years. In 1997, the government hired British mercenaries to fight the rebellion. The head of the mercenaries told the government that one of his companies could buy the Panguna mine later.

The Papua New Guinea Defence Forces stopped the mercenaries. This was a type of rebellion in Papua New Guinea. It did not remove the government but it did start the peace process in Bougainville.

## For you to try

Collect information about Bougainville and discuss the following questions.

- What benefits does Bougainville gain by staying part of Papua New Guinea?
- How does your province compare to Bougainville?
- If Bougainville became completely independent, would it be a strong state, an emerging state or a fragile state?

## Future development in the Pacific Islands

As we have seen, government in the Pacific Islands has had three main periods: traditional, colonial and independent. The traditional period started as long ago as 50 000 years. It changed, adapted and survived in many places. In only a few places, it did not do so well. Colonial government often helped the coloniser and hurt the colonised. Groups from larger populations continue to move into areas of smaller, weaker populations. The latest group is from China and other parts of Asia who are replacing some Europeans in the Pacific. Independent government is much newer. It has failed in some places.

All Pacific Island populations are growing. For the region, the rate is somewhere between 2.2 to 2.7 per cent every year. Eventually it must slow down. Growing populations result in growing population densities.

Most Pacific Island countries have few resources. Papua New Guinea and Fiji, however, are two examples of countries that have plenty of resources. Both have seen political fighting over the resources. Both have had complaints about corruption and injustice. Many people are still waiting to see the benefits from government organisation.

## Resources and organisation of some Pacific countries

Read about the resources and organisation of the Pacific countries on the following pages. When you have finished reading, complete the activities on pages 83 and 84.

# Fiji

## Resources

- arable land (land that is good for agriculture)
- plenty of fresh water
- tourism (300 000 to 400 000 tourists annually)
- resources: sugar (with access to European Union markets), gold, fish, timber, molasses, coconut oil
- garment industry (in decline)

## Organisation

- series of coups or threats of coups have weakened government and hurt tourism
- population growing faster than employment opportunities
- tension between indigenous Fijians and Indo-Fijian

## Kiribati

### Resources

- total land: 700 sq km
- limited arable land (2.7% of total land)
- resources: fish, copra, phosphate (little left on Banaba Island), tourism
- crops must be protected from land crabs
- water is scarce and polluted
- soils are poor

### Organisation

- government slow to address population issues
- government has not opened many opportunities for economic growth
- little money in Reserve Fund for emergencies
- shortage of skilled workers

## Solomon Islands

### Resources

- total land: 27 500 sq km
- 580 sq km arable land
- resources: timber, fish, palm oil, copra, lead, zinc, nickel, bauxite
- highest population growth in Pacific (up 2.9% per year)

### Organisation

- a weak and corrupt government has led to fighting (Australian armed forces restored peace)
- government is now working on recovery, reform and development, with Australian assistance

## Tonga

### Resources

- total land: 750 sq km
- arable land: 480 sq km
- Tongans good at changing agriculture products for market
- exports: pumpkin, fish, coconut, vanilla beans
- small manufacturing centre

### Organisation

- monarchy under pressure to introduce more democratic reforms
- government is trying to develop the private sector in hopes of increasing business

## Tuvula

### Resources

- total land: 26 sq km
- exports: fish, garments, copra
- little arable land
- poor soil
- little drinkable water
- government major employer in a total population of 11 000 people

### Organisation

- government very dependent on international assistance

## Vanuatu

### Resources

- total land: 12 000 sq km
- arable land: 1500 sq km
- limited drinkable water
- exports: tourism, timber, cattle, copra, cacao

### Organisation

- factions and clan interests have weakened government
- government aims to increase tourism and agriculture (especially livestock)

## For you to make

Copy this page and create an information sheet by finding information about your province. You can find information by asking people in your community, reading newspapers, getting government brochures, etc.

- Find out about the resources and organisation for your province. Find photographs or draw pictures to illustrate your information.

Name of your province: ____________________

**Resources:**

**Organisation:**

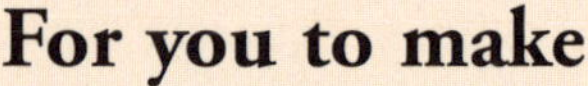

## For you to make

Copy this page and create an information sheet by finding information about Papua New Guinea. You can find information by asking people in your community, reading newspapers, getting government brochures, etc.

- Find out about the resources and organisation for Papua New Guinea. Find photographs or draw pictures to illustrate your information.

## Papua New Guinea

**Resources:**

**Organisation:**

# 3
# Culture

## Chapter summary

In this chapter you will have the opportunity to:

✓ identify and describe some features of national cultures

✓ discuss similarities and differences in Papua New Guinea and other Pacific Island cultures

✓ identify changes that are happening in national cultures

✓ consider the meaning of Independence Day and ways to celebrate it.

## Syllabus references

Strand: Culture

Sub-strand: National and regional cultures

Outcomes

**7.3.1** Students are able to identify and describe key elements of national cultures.

**7.3.2** Students are able to appraise the main influences that contribute to national cultures.

**7.3.3** Students are able to participate in national culture.

# What is culture?

Culture is the total way that people live. It is created by groups of human beings. Everywhere you look you can see parts of culture. There are many different cultures. Cultures overlap, cultures borrow from each other, cultures adapt and innovate, and cultures are always changing.

*Pacific culture* is a term that covers many different ideas and ways. It can include other cultures like Melanesian, Micronesian and Polynesian cultures. Again, each of these cultures also includes many more cultures, such as Motuan, Sepik, Samoan, Engan or Hawaiian.

All nations, all over the world, have certain things that define their culture. They include such things as:

- language
- music and dance
- food and cooking
- customs and traditions
- myths and stories.
- arts and crafts (such as paintings, pottery, weapons, tools)
- clothing and personal decoration
- laws
- taboos

How do we learn our culture? Most people begin to learn their culture when they are born. Babies learn their language from their parents, family, elders and community. As we grow up, we learn more about our culture. When we move to other places, we learn about other cultures and perhaps borrow some of the features of those cultures.

## For you to try

- Choose a part of culture you find interesting (such as music, art, law or language) and make a chart comparing your culture with another. How are they similar? How are they different?
- Think of a culture that is very different from yours (such as American or Australian). How is this culture different from yours?

# Examining culture

You can look at culture in many different ways. You can compare different themes in Pacific culture. There are hundreds of ways to look at culture in the Pacific.

Culture is changing in Papua New Guinea and across the Pacific Islands. Some of these changes are good and some are bad. But how do we tell when cultural change is good or bad? How do we judge this?

We can look at particular aspects of culture (such as those listed on page 54) and ask ourselves whether traditional culture is something to be treasured and kept or whether it should change or adapt.

As you read through this chapter, think about the aspects of traditional culture that you think you should keep and which aspects of new culture you should accept. For example, is it good to give up your village ceremonies or should you keep them? Why?

The following pages show twelve different themes for you to study and explore through pictures. Look at the pictures and analyse what they are telling you about the cultures shown. What values, ideas, adaptations and innovations do they show? What do they tell you about how culture is changing in the Pacific?

## Rural people

In Papua New Guinea and many other parts of the Pacific, most people are rural. How are these cultures changing? How are they staying the same?

## Schools and religious places

What roles do schools have in culture? What parts of culture do schools represent? What are the roles of religious places in cultures? What do different religious buildings tell us about cultures?

## Traditional cultural performances in the Pacific

What does *traditional* mean? What cultural values are expressed in these performances? Compare Papua New Guinea traditional cultural performances with the other Pacific examples. What do they have in common? What is different?

## Raising children

Populations are growing everywhere in the Pacific. The ways of raising children reflect many parts of a culture. How are you being raised? Compare your experiences with the children in these pictures. What parts of cultures do you all have? What is different?

## Traditional artefacts and change

This is just one small selection of traditional artefacts and changes. What is changing the culture to change artefacts? How quickly has this happened where you are? What story do these different artefacts tell about Pacific cultures?

## Urban settlements

Urban settlement almost completely changes a traditional culture. Design and structure change. New systems are introduced. What else can you find that is new in urban culture? What can you find that still reflects Pacific cultures? Or does Pacific culture include a new urban culture?

## Markets

Here are blends of cultures. Again what is new, what is adapted and what is the same in many Pacific markets? Think about where the sellers and their products come from and answer what that tells you about cultures. Do the same for the buyers and where the goods go.

## Remnants of war

Traditional warfare has a very long tradition in the Pacific. Modern warfare has a much shorter history. The landscape is left with a few remains of modern warfare. What impacts has it had on Papua New Guinea culture?

## Rural economic activities

A major change with traditional cultures is the introduction of cash. How are rural activities changing culture? How are they changing values?

## Food

Food is very important in Pacific cultures. Preparing and sharing food have many meanings in different types of cultural situations. Compare these pictures to your own cultural practices.

## Transportation

Traditional Pacific cultures have based transportation on walking and different types of canoes. How many different ways can you find where transportation is changing cultures?

## Settlement and housing

Settlement and housing reflect many parts of culture. What are these pictures telling you about Pacific culture?

## For you to try

- Now go back over the different pictures. Try to find different themes that can also tell you more about Papua New Guinea and Pacific cultures. For example, look at the differences in the roles of men and women. What does this theme tell you? What other themes can you find? Explore and discuss them in class.
- Another theme about Papua New Guinea is how we celebrate Independence Day. What do these pictures tell you about that? What is missing? Draw or collect your own pictures to show different ways to celebrate Independence Day.

# 4

# Integrating Projects

## Chapter summary

In this chapter you will have the opportunity to:

✓ use the social science process

✓ look at national and regional needs

## Syllabus references

Strand: Integrating projects

Sub-strand: Improving provincial and national communities and societies

Outcomes

**7.4.1** Use the social science process to describe the province and compare ways to improve the life of the province

**7.4.2** Use the social science process to describe the nation and to propose ways for Papua New Guinea to be more involved in the region

# The social science process

Now it is time for you to do your own studies. In this final chapter, you will use the social science process to study parts of your province, the nation and other countries in the region. You can choose different topics. You can look at different problems. You can suggest solutions to improve the province, nation or region. You will need the social science process to do this.

### For you to try

As a class, discuss what you understand and remember about the social science process before you start the review of the social science process.

- How do you think that the social science process can be used to look at parts of your province, the nation or the region? Discuss examples for each of the following:
  - the environment
  - natural resources
  - other resources (how many other resources can you think of?)
  - social organisation
  - culture
  - other aspects.

  (Each of the items listed above are related. For example, you could discuss how culture affects the natural environment in the province, or how the natural environment affects culture in the province.)
- How many different examples can you think of where we can use the social science process in the province, nation or region?

# Review of the social science process

Now, let us review the social science process. Then you can use the social science process to study provincial, national and regional issues. You can offer solutions to problems in your conclusions.

## Observation

The social science process starts with observation. That means looking and hearing. It can include reading and studying information. To understand what is happening in Papua New Guinea and the region, you will need to find information. You can do this by:

- talking and listening to people
- reading newspapers and books
- listening to radio
- watching television if you are in a place that has television

What other ways can you find information?

When you observe something, you frequently will want to ask questions about what you have seen or heard. "Why did this happen?" or "How could this be made better?" are the sorts of questions that scientists ask themselves. These questions can lead to a **hypothesis**, such as "I think this happened because ..." or "This could be made better by ..." The idea or question will provide you with a topic to study.

**Choose a topic**: For example, you think about what is happening in the province, nation or region. This will lead you to ask a question. You decide on a topic from your observations of what is in the news or books or radio or from people.

**Gather information**: Next you have to carefully gather information about your topic. You can find some types of national and regional information on the radio and in newspapers. Books are another good source. You can ask people, too. Remember to consider attitudes and values when you do this.

**Evaluate the information**: This is a very important part of the process. You have to look at your information and analyse it carefully. You need to find out what it means. Remember to consider the attitudes and values of the people who gave the information. Remember to look for bias and prejudice. Your evaluation will be your written report.

**Make conclusions**: Finally, you need to make conclusions. You will study your written report. The last thing you will write will be the conclusion. The conclusion will tell what you have found. For example:

- What is the answer to the study question? (Maybe your hypothesis was right or wrong. Your conclusion tells us about this.)
- What solutions are there for the study problems?
- What is the best solution?
- Can we predict what will happen in the future?
- Is the information partly correct?
- What can now be done?

**Further study or follow-up studies**: Many parts of social science change quickly. You can observe, evaluate and make conclusions about an issue. Then social organisation or culture or resources change and the study will change. Only follow-up studies will tell you what is happening.

# Examples of studies using the social science process

There are many issues in social science for study. You will find many looking at your province, the nation and the region.

There are many ways to do social science studies. Let us look at some examples of how to do these studies. Each class will have different resources. You will have to adapt and innovate in your studies.

## A An example of social organisation

*What is the role of provinces in the nation?*

**Choose a topic**: You notice that people are talking about one type of social organisation: the provinces. You see in newspapers that there are questions about provinces. You find a number or questions such as:

- Why have provinces?
- What is good about provinces?
- What is bad about provinces?
- What other systems could there be if we had no provinces?

You decide to study this issue. For example, you might title the study, "Is Having Provinces Good for the Nation?" You make a plan for how to do the study.

**Gather information**: You talk to people in your province about their ideas. You could make up a questionnaire to be sure you asked the same questions of all people. You could study the newspapers and listen to the radio for people's ideas about provinces.

**Evaluate the information**: You consider all the information you have gathered. What does it mean? You analyse the values and attitudes you find in the information. You discuss what you have found with others. You write a report.

**Make conclusions**: You write a conclusion at the end of your report. It may provide an answer to the study question or it may only give a partial answer. This depends on the information you have collected. Sometimes you cannot give a complete answer because your information is limited.

**Further study or follow-up studies**: Questions about the social organisation of nations will always be asked. Culture, resources and other things will change. There will always be a need for follow-up studies for questions about having or not having provinces.

## B An example of culture

*Is urban settlement changing the cultures in the Pacific region?*

**Choose a topic**: You notice that many old people are saying that urban settlements are completely changing Melanesian cultures. You find a magazine article about cities changing the Pacific way. You hear a radio program about Honolulu in Hawaii having destroyed the old Hawaiian Polynesian culture. You think of questions such as:

- Are cities completely changing the Pacific?
- Does Port Moresby have a new urban culture?
- What is happening to traditional culture in urban areas?
- Is cultural change good or bad?
- Are cities hurting or helping people?

You decide to study this issue. You see that there are many values and attitudes about rural and urban cultures. You know you will have to be careful when looking at these different values. You make a plan for your study that you decide to call "How Are Cities Changing Our Culture?"

**Gather information**: You talk to people about their experience in rural and urban places. Again, you could make up a questionnaire. It might be different for rural and urban people. You can study resources such as books and newspapers, and listen to the radio for information. You could look at the pictures in Chapter 3 of this book and collect many of your own for analysis

**Evaluate the information**: You consider all the information you have gathered. You are very careful to analyse the values and attitudes you find in the information. For example: Why do some people say cities and urban culture is bad? Why do some say it is good? Who tells us what is bad or good in a culture? You discuss what you have found with others. You write a report.

**Make conclusions**: The conclusion is your opinion. You state what values you have used and what values you have studied.

**Further study or follow-up studies**: Questions about culture will always be asked. Culture is always changing so there will be further studies. Maybe you will read them later and think, "Well I made a study about that too!"

## C An example of resource study

*What is the best role for agricultural exports in the Pacific?*

**Choose a topic**: You notice that people are talking about lower prices for coconuts or vanilla or chillies. You read that Tonga and Vanuatu smallholders have slowed or stopped coconut or vanilla production. You find a number of questions such as:

- Why were vanilla prices very high before, but are now low?
- Should Papua New Guinea be growing coconuts or spices or something else?
- Why are exports important?
- What happens if a nation has no agricultural exports?
- What Pacific countries rely on agricultural exports?
- What other ways are there to earn money in the rural parts of the Pacific?

You decide to study this issue. For example, you might title the study, "Are Coconuts a Good Export for Papua New Guinea?" or, if you have more information, "Are Coconuts a Good Export for the Pacific?"

**Gather information**: You talk to growers, exporters and other business people. You ask the old people about what they remember of the coconut industry. You look for written information on copra or vanilla or whatever crop you have chosen.

**Evaluate the information**: Consider all the information. Analyse the information carefully. Discuss it with others. Then you write a report.

**Make conclusions**: You write a conclusion based on the body of your report.

**Further study or follow-up studies**: These will continue with agriculture.

## D An example of social organisation and culture

*Should primary schools be run by the government or by churches?*

**Choose a topic**: You read a newspaper article about church-based schools. You find that the article has a strong attitude about schools and churches. This raises a number or questions such as:

- What are the roles of primary schools and what are their most important roles?
- Are churches the best organisations to run primary schools?
- Should all primary schools be government primary schools?
- Can churches provide more resources to primary schools?
- Can national and provincial governments provide more resources to primary schools?

You decide to study this issue. For example, you might title the study, "Should Churches Run Our Primary Schools?" or, "Should Provincial and National Governments Run Primary Schools?"

**Gather information**: You talk to people in education. You talk to different church leaders and different school leaders. You could also talk to students and teachers (and parents if you have time) in church schools and in government schools.

**Evaluate the information**: You consider all the information you have gathered. You will find many values and attitudes in this information. You discuss what you have found with others. You write a report.

**Make conclusions**: You write a conclusion based on the body of your report.

**Further study or follow-up studies**: These will continue with education issues.

## E An example of changes to cultures, resources and social organisation

*What is the impact of new transportation systems?*

**Choose a topic**: A car hits a young child. The child dies in this road accident. It happens near you in the city. An elderly woman is walking alongside the highway. She lives in your rural area. A passing vehicle kills her. The driver does not stop. The driver leaves her to die alone.

You see articles in the newspaper about people being killed by cars and trucks in Papua New Guinea. Many people are talking. They say that people drive too fast. They say people don't care. They say pedestrians should have safer places to walk. You find a number of questions such as:

- Are too many resources going to roads and not enough for pedestrians?
- Have drivers forgotten Melanesian values when driving?
- Are pedestrians unsafe in Papua New Guinea?
- Are road systems safe in Pacific island countries?
- How can road safety be improved?

You decide to study this issue. For example, you might title the study, "How Can We Stop Pedestrian Deaths?"

**Gather information**: You talk to police, pedestrians, drivers, road engineers and anyone else who knows about road safety and road issues. You read whatever material you can find on this problem. You look for statistics about road deaths in Papua New Guinea and the Pacific.

**Evaluate the information**: You consider all the information you have gathered. You think carefully about any statistics you have gathered. How reliable are they? Do the police and others keep good records? You consider what cultural values and attitudes are changing. You look at adaptation and innovation in the way transport is used in Papua New Guinea. You discuss what you have found with others. You write a report.

**Make conclusions**: You write a conclusion based on the body of your report.

**Further study or follow-up studies**: These will continue with road accidents and pedestrian deaths.

## For you to try

Now it is your turn to do a study. The topic can be about any aspect of the following areas for Papua New Guinea or another place in the region:

- the environment
- natural resources
- other resources (how many other resources can you think of?)
- social organisation
- culture

You might follow up some part of the examples already given. You might find articles or listen to information from the radio or listen to people around you for other ideas. The key is to use the social science process to help find answers to questions you have.

On the following pages are extracts from two articles. They are just examples that could be the base for a social science study. Look at the attitudes and values in the articles. What questions and studies do they raise?

You can find many more articles, pictures and other information to study. There are also many others in this text that you can follow for ideas.

Now apply the social science process and make your study!

# The Indian Factor

## Why more and more are leaving the islands

By Michael Field

Huddled together, looking cold with fear, a group of Fiji Indians stood on the empty street of Korovou one afternoon in 2000. Make-shift bags at their feet, they waited for a bus to take them to Suva, 50 kilometres south.

Armed with military weapons, rebels had seized Korovou in support of local boy George Speight who was holding hostage the government of Prime Minister Mahendra Chaudhry.

Days earlier in a Rewa River valley, where Indians had grown vegetables for nearly a century, 16-year-old Romika Nair told of gangs looting, burning and assaulting Indians.

Five years on from the third coup to afflict Fiji since 1987, the real price is emerging. Over 100 000 Indians have left for New Zealand, Australia, Canada and the United States since 1987; a stunning loss in a talent-short country of just 900 000. Even the talented indigenous people are leaving.

A tragic story lies in the past and Indians suffer still the myth that they are somehow to blame for Fiji's chronic instability.

Indo-Fijians are mostly descendents of indentured labourers brought in by the British to work on CSR Australia-owned sugar plantations. Between 1879 and 1916 around 60 000 "girmitiyas" came. All first stayed on Nukulau Island—Speight's prison today—for quarantine purposes.

When the indentured labour system ended, a small but sizeable group of Punjab farmers and Gujerati merchants came, creating a casteless patchwork of Tamils, Nepalese, North Indians, Sikhs and Bengalis—all speaking a kind of pidgin Hindi.

Like Pakeha New Zealanders, Fiji Indians suffer an identity issue. Professor Lal [an academic born in India] insists he's Indo-Fijian. "My grandfather's country is not mine," adding that for his children India is "essentially a strange place full of strange people."

In the 1966 census, Indians accounted for 51 per cent of the population, Fiji Island Bureau of Statistics says. Indigenous Fijians were just 42 per cent—the rest made up of Chinese, Europeans, Rotumans and other Pacific Islanders.

London colonial masters feared Indians would take over the country and in a long and complicated process—

which continues today in the electoral system—measures were taken to ensure indigenous Fijians would never lose their land in the way the Maori had in New Zealand, and that their political supremacy would remain intact.

Following independence in 1970, and under Prime Minister Ratu Sir Kamisese Mara, this happened. But in 1987 the Indo-Fijian dominated Fiji Labour Party (FLP) won power under Prime Minister Timoci Bavadra. That prompted the military's number three, Sitiveni Rabuka, to stage two coups.

Promising a Taukei or indigenous government, he instituted a racist constitution—producing the first wave of Indo-Fijian emigration. By 1999, even Rabuka had recognised the heavy cost and brought in the multi-racial constitution and a re-organised preferential voting system, albeit still on racial lines. That led to another FLP victory, this time with Chaudhry, although heading a cabinet dominated by indigenous Fijians.

A year later came Speight's coup and then military commander Voreqe Baininarama's martial law—a coup in everything but name. Indo-Fijians were revealed as nothing more than a stalking horse for indigenous tribal warfare.

In Fiji, no one knows for sure what is happening; Fiji last had a census 10 years ago and migration cards in recipient countries don't record race.

Fiji's statistics bureau estimates the population at December 2004 at 840 201, including 320 659 Indians, approximately 38 per cent of the total population. In 2000, Indians were 41 per cent of the population.

The radical change is shown in the way the bureau estimates how long it would take a population to double in size. In 1986, it reckoned the indigenous population would double in 29 years and the Indians in 40 years. In 1996, the figure was 39 years for indigenous, and never for Indians—minus 241 years.

Rajenda Prasad, a former town clerk of Ba, on the northern cost of Viti Levu, says India has almost no significance for Indo-Fijians.

"In my conscience when the term 'home' is used, what comes to mind is Fiji, not India."

But Indo-Fijians live with the painful dilemma.

"Our people have experienced through the coups and politicise of the government that we are not wanted."

Most who leave, come to the "grim conclusion that Fiji will not be secure and stable for them in the future." They do well in New Zealand.

"At least they don't have to live with the trauma of Fiji. Fiji is an illusion, a nightmare for most. But in their heart Fiji is still magnetic."

# Fragile States

In the Pacific region, public administration is often weak, business enterprises face considerable hurdles and precious natural resources are not managed sustainability.

In a few cases, corruption within government is impeding progress. Even where good governance and stability prevail, many small island nations face poor growth prospects because of their size and relative isolation. Their circumstances of geography shut them out of many economic opportunities arising from increased global trade and investment. The tiny islands of Kiribati and Tuvalu also face daunting environmental challenges that further undermine their viability.

The newly independent nation of East Timor has the will, but not yet the capacity, to ensure its institutions function well. Other countries, such as Vanuatu, show continued political instability, including frequent leadership changes, which undermines a long-term commitment to good governance and economic reform.

The administration of some Pacific nations is so frail that governments are unable to deliver basic services to large section of their populations. For example, water supplied may be erratic, sanitation systems not properly maintained and power supplies unreliable. Always it's the poorest people who suffer most.

Poverty mixed with weak government can be a disastrous combination. Where people are poorly paid, and the administration is weak and lacking in adequate checks and balances, opportunities for corruption multiply.

Nations that reach this level of vulnerability are characterised as 'fragile states'. Such nations have little chance of overcoming such serious problems alone. In fact, if left unassisted, they may experience fragility and development stagnation for generations.

Aid, for fragile states is enormously important and far more difficult. The reasons for this are complex and various but usually include one or more of the following:

- instability or open conflict
- weak administration systems vulnerable to corruption
- small size and geographical isolation.

Australia is helping to drive renewed international efforts to bring about reforms in fragile states. It's also taking a new approach to aid delivery which, in contrast with previous decades, is much broader and comprehensive.

Australia's new approach favours, for example, strong equal working partnerships with recipient governments and their communities. It calls for sensitivity, flexibility and cultural knowledge. Yet passive acceptance of help is not enough for, as Australia and other donors have learnt, reforms will only be successful if they are welcomed, trusted and have the recipient country's full backing.

*From* Focus, *June–August 2005*

# Glossary

| | |
|---|---|
| **archipelago** | a group or collection of several islands |
| **Australia** | a large island continent and country located in the Southern Hemisphere |
| **border** | the imaginary line dividing countries, provinces, nations, etc. |
| **cardinal points** | the primary points of a compass showing direction: north, south, east and west |
| **colonial** | a word describing anything about a colony |
| **colony** | a place (such as an island) that is controlled by another country |
| **constitution** | a legal document defining the basic legal rights, responsibilities and functions of a nation's government |
| **coup** | the quick and usually violent change of power within a country; usually by the overthrowing of an elected government (also called a coup d'état) |
| **culture** | everything social or learned by human beings, including such things as beliefs, the arts, social organisation and language |
| **democracy** | a system of government where the people elect leaders and other representatives by voting |
| **development** | the practice of improving things (making them better or more productive) |
| **elected official** | a person chosen by the people to fill a governmental role |
| **election** | the process of choosing officials to represent people |
| **environment** | all of the physical things (either natural or made by people) in a particular place |
| **gene** | a thing that determines characteristics passed on from parent to child |
| **genetics** | the study of genes |
| **hypothesis** | a reasonable idea or question on which research can be based |
| **independence** | not being dependent on another person or country; freedom from another country's power or authority |
| **Indonesia** | a Southeast Asian country that shares a land border with Papua New Guinea; includes the main islands of Sumatra, Java, Timor, Sulawesi, the Moluccas, parts of the islands of Borneo and New Guinea, and many smaller islands |
| **island** | a body of land entirely surrounded by water, including sand cays, volcanic islands, atolls and sedimentary islands |

**nation** — an independent country, such as Papua New Guinea or Australia; can also be called a country or state

**natural hazard** — a danger found in the physical environment, such as volcanic eruptions, flooding, cyclones, land slips and frosts

**New Guinea** — an island in the southwest Pacific, with part of Indonesia on the western half, and a large part of the nation of Papua New Guinea

**ocean** — a large body of salt water; the major oceans are the Antarctic, the Arctic, the Pacific, the Atlantic and the Indian

**population density** — the number of people living in a certain area, such as a square kilometre

**province** — a political unit found in some countries; a province covers a designated territory and provides services that the national government may not provide

**public servant** — a person employed by a government to provide services for the people of a nation, state, province, or other administrative area

**region** — a large territory that will have some things in common, such as culture, environment or shared history.

**resource** — anything of use to human beings, such as water, schools, plants, minerals, clean air, etc., that is needed for social, physical, economic or political development

**scale** — a measurement based on a ratio, such as 1:100 (which means one unit on paper equals 100 actual things)

**settlement pattern** — a description that shows how people have moved to and settled in a particular region or place; settlement patterns often reflect the resources of a particular place

**social science** — the study of human behaviour, culture and society

**sovereign** — independent; a sovereign state is a country that is not ruled by another country

**state** — any political unit, such as a country or province; can also mean a state (like a province) within a country, such as the United States of America

**sustainable** — able to be kept going; a sustainable resource is a resource that is managed so that it not used until it is all gone

**transport system** — a way of moving people and things from one place to another; transport systems can be complex or simple

**West Papua** — the Indonesian half of the island of New Guinea; also known as Western New Guinea

# Acknowledgments

The author and publisher wish to thank the following copyright holders for granting permission to reproduce their material. Sources are as follows:

AAP Images, pp. 39, 58, 68, 79 (bottom); Photograph courtesy of the Anthropology Photographic Archive, Department of Anthropology, University of Auckland http://www.library.auckland.ac.nz/databases/learn_database/public.asp?record=apa, p. 22; Photographs courtesy of Crawford House, pp. 9, 34, 75; Fotolia, p. 80 (bottom); Photograph courtesy of Tony Lolkes de Beer, p. 41; iStock Photography, pp. 31, 42, 44, 80 (top right), 81 (top left); Jupiter Images, pp. 77 (top left and right), 78 (bottom), 79 (top left and right), 80 (top left); Photolibrary, pp. 77 (bottom), 78 (top right), 82 (top right and bottom); Travel-Images.com, p. 73.

Every effort has been made to trace the original source of copyright material contained in this book. The publisher would be pleased to hear from copyright holders to rectify any errors or omissions.